Updates to Watershed Modeling in the Potholes Reservoir Basin, Washington—a Supplement to Scientific Investigations Report 2009–5081

By Mark Mastin

Open File Report 2012–1251

U.S. Department of the Interior
U.S. Geological Survey

U.S. Department of the Interior
KEN SALAZAR, Secretary

U.S. Geological Survey
Marcia K. McNutt, Director

U.S. Geological Survey, Reston, Virginia: 2012

For more information on the USGS—the Federal source for science about the Earth,
its natural and living resources, natural hazards, and the environment—visit
http://www.usgs.gov or call 1–888–ASK–USGS

For an overview of USGS information products, including maps, imagery, and publications,
visit *http://www.usgs.gov/pubprod*

To order this and other USGS information products, visit *http://store.usgs.gov*

Suggested citation:
Mastin, M.C, 2012, Updates to watershed modeling in the Potholes Reservoir basin, Washington—a supplement to
Scientific Investigation Report 2009-5081: U.S. Geological Survey Open-File Report 2012-1251, 52 p.

Contents

Figures

Tables

Conversion Factors

Inch/Pound to SI

Multiply	By	To obtain
	Length	
inch (in.)	2.54	centimeter (cm)
foot (ft)	0.3048	meter (m)
	Area	
acre	4,047	square meter (m^2)
	Volume	
cubic foot (ft^3)	0.02832	cubic meter (m^3)
acre-foot (acre-ft)	1,233	cubic meter (m^3)
	Flow rate	
cubic foot per second (ft^3/s)	0.02832	Cubic meter per second (m^3/s)

Temperature in degrees Fahrenheit (°F) may be converted to degrees Celsius (°C) as follows:
°C=(°F-32)/1.8
Temperature in degrees Celsius (°C) may be converted to degrees Fahrenheit (°F) as follows:
°F=(1.8×°C)+32

Datums

Vertical coordinate information is referenced to the "North American Vertical Datum of 1988 (NAVD 88)."
Horizontal coordinate information is referenced to the "North American Datum of 1983 (NAD 83)."
Elevation, as used in this report, refers to distance above the vertical datum.

Updates to Watershed Modeling in the Potholes Reservoir Basin, Washington—a Supplement to Scientific Investigations Report 2009–5081

By Mark Mastin

Abstract

A previous collaborative effort between the U.S. Geological Survey and the Bureau of Reclamation resulted in a watershed model for four watersheds that discharge into Potholes Reservoir, Washington. Since the model was constructed, two new meteorological sites have been established that provide more reliable real-time information. The Bureau of Reclamation was interested in incorporating this new information into the existing watershed model developed in 2009, and adding measured snowpack information to update simulated results and to improve forecasts of runoff. This report includes descriptions of procedures to aid a user in making model runs, including a description of the Object User Interface for the watershed model with details on specific keystrokes to generate model runs for the contributing basins. A new real-time, data-gathering computer program automates the creation of the model input files and includes the new meteorological sites. The 2009 watershed model was updated with the new sites and validated by comparing simulated results to measured data. As in the previous study, the updated model (2012 model) does a poor job of simulating individual storms, but a reasonably good job of simulating seasonal runoff volumes. At three streamflow-gaging stations, the January 1 to June 30 retrospective forecasts of runoff volume for years 2010 and 2011 were within 40 percent of the measured runoff volume for five of the six comparisons, ranging from -39.4 to 60.3 percent difference. A procedure for collecting measured snowpack data and using the data in the watershed model for forecast model runs, based on the Ensemble Streamflow Prediction method, is described, with an example that uses 2004 snow-survey data.

Introduction

Since 2002, the U.S. Geological Survey (USGS) Washington Water Science Center has been working with the Ephrata, Washington, office of the Bureau of Reclamation (Reclamation) to develop a watershed model of the drainage basins that drain into Potholes Reservoir, Washington, in four streams: Rocky Ford Creek, Crab Creek, Rocky Coulee, and Lind Coulee. Previous work in these basins includes the development of a watershed model using the USGS Precipitation-Runoff Modeling System (Leavesley and others, 1983) that incorporates a graphical user interface to facilitate user operation, and a USGS report (Mastin, 2009) that documents the model. The model has been installed on computers at the Reclamation office in Ephrata, and the USGS provided training in its use.

Reclamation manages the Columbia Basin Project, a multipurpose project that provides hydropower, recreation, irrigation, and flood protection. Pumps move water from Franklin D. Roosevelt Lake to Banks Lake for irrigation through canals to farmlands located mostly south of Banks Lake, and to feed Potholes Reservoir, which regulates discharges for irrigation of more lands farther south of the reservoir (fig. 1). Potholes Reservoir also receives runoff from the streams that feed Moses Lake, whose outflow feeds directly into Potholes Reservoir, and from Lind Coulee, which discharges directly into Potholes Reservoir (fig. 1). Management of this water-conveyance system may be improved if the natural spring runoff can be projected months or weeks in advance with real-time forecasts based on historical weather information and the current hydrologic conditions in the basin. Additionally, long-term studies of the hydrology of the system generally need historical runoff information that may not be available from the existing streamflow-gaging network. For these reasons, a set of watershed models (model units Crab Creek, including Rocky Ford Creek, Lind Coulee, and Rocky Coulee) was created as part of the original study to facilitate Reclamation's water-conveyance decision-making process by providing forecasted and historical runoff information that affects the inflows to Potholes Reservoir. A group of long-term meteorological sites provides daily precipitation and daily minimum and maximum temperatures as input (file, pot_lt.data; see appendix A for more information on input files) to the set of long-term models. Not all the long-term meteorological sites have real-time telemetry, so the same model (that is, same process algorithms) is used with a slightly different group of meteorological sites that have real-time telemetry. Therefore, the real-time model uses a different input file (pot_rt.data) than the long-term model.

After working for several years with the model developed in 2009, Reclamation and the USGS discovered a few shortcomings and looked for ways to improve the real-time simulations. For example, the existing network of real-time meteorological and soil moisture sites included fewer sites than the number of sites used to calibrate the initial model, and incomplete data were collected at some of those sites. Since the initial model was completed, two new meteorological sites, Almira and Davenport (fig. 2), were added to the network as Agrimet sites. The Almira and Davenport sites include monitoring of soil moisture and soil temperature, along with air temperature and precipitation. Agrimet is a satellite-based network of automated agricultural weather stations throughout the Pacific Northwest operated and maintained by Reclamation (Bureau of Reclamation, 2012a). The data collected by the new sites are maintained on the Hydromet real-time database system, a network of automated hydrological and meteorological monitoring systems also operated by Reclamation (Bureau of Reclamation, 2012b). Soil moisture and soil temperature are not inputs to the model, but provide useful information for the modeler. For example, frozen ground has the important function of dramatically increasing runoff during rain storms and soil-temperature information allows the modeler to monitor whether the model is correctly simulating frozen or non-frozen soil. Similarly, the ability of the model to simulate snow volumes accurately in the watershed at the time runoff forecasts are made is critical to the success of the forecasts. A modeler can distribute measured snow-water equivalents to the hydrologic modeling units that represent the watershed and substitute the information for simulated snow conditions to improve runoff forecasts.

Detailed information about the Potholes watershed model is available in the previously published model (hereafter called the "2009 model") documentation (Mastin, 2009). Some details about the file names, flow-routing schematics, and model setup are available in appendix A of this report.

Purpose and Scope

The purpose of this report is to document changes to the previously published Potholes watershed 2009 model, to provide instructions for model use, and to describe protocols for collecting snowpack data in the watershed. This report specifically documents 1) the updated model parameters for new sets of input data from the two new meteorological sites, 2) verification of the updated model using the two new sites, 3) the upgraded real-time data retrieval program that includes the two new meteorological sites, 4) a guide for making snow measurements in the Potholes Reservoir basin to determine snow-water equivalents, and 5) the method used to update the watershed model with measured snow-water equivalents.

Updating the Watershed Model to Incorporate Two New Meteorological Sites

Two new meteorological sites (fig. 2), one near Almira and one on the Wilke Experimental Farm in Davenport, were installed in January 2009 to provide meteorological and hydrological information in the headwaters of the Crab Creek basin to improve runoff simulations from the Potholes Watershed Model.

The 2009 real-time model uses the National Weather Service (NWS) meteorological site at Davenport (NWS index number 2007), a Hydromet site at Dry Falls, and seven other meteorological sites. The NWS site at Davenport often was unreliable in providing real-time data and the Dry Falls site was located outside the watershed boundaries. The new Hydromet sites, Davenport and Almira (fig. 2), continuously monitor real-time air temperature, precipitation, soil temperature, and soil moisture.

It is important to have reliable, real-time meteorological sites because one of the purposes of the model is to forecast the upcoming runoff season (usually February through July) based on current watershed conditions. The watershed model uses daily maximum and minimum air temperature and daily precipitation as inputs. To simulate current conditions, the model must have current daily inputs; therefore, real-time, daily minimum and maximum air temperature and precipitation are needed.

Soil temperature and soil moisture are not inputs to the watershed model, but they provide indicators for comparison with watershed-model simulation results. Measured and simulated soil moisture can be compared to give the user an indication of the reliability of the model. A similar comparison can be made between measured and simulated soil temperature. Soil temperature indicates whether the soil is frozen. The pathway of runoff can change substantially depending on whether the ground is frozen or not frozen (Mastin, 2009). The watershed model uses a simple threshold-type index to simulate frozen ground. Once the threshold is exceeded, all water available for runoff or infiltration is routed to the surface runoff pathway and quickly becomes runoff. This closure of the infiltration pathway for available water can result in dramatically high peak discharges with little input from snowmelt and precipitation. If the index is in agreement with the soil information measured at the new sites, a user will have more confidence in the runoff volumes forecasted by the model.

The updated model (hereafter called the "2012 model") was developed by creating a new parameter file to accommodate the new meteorological sites used for input to the model—Agrimet sites Davenport and Almira, in place of the Davenport NWS site and the Dry Falls Hydromet site. The location parameters for Almira were substituted for the Dry Falls location parameters and the location and mean monthly precipitation parameters were left the same for the two Davenport sites. These location parameters include the temperature station latitude, longitude (Universal Transverse Mercator [UTM], zone 11 coordinates), and elevation (feet) (model parameters tsta_ylat, tsta_xlong, and tsta_elev, respectively), and the precipitation station latitude and longitude (model parameters psta_ylat, and psta_xlong, respectively). One more precipitation parameter, psta_mon, which represents the long-term monthly precipitation at the meteorological site, was estimated from the 1961-90 mean monthly precipitation at Almira simulated by the Parameter-elevation Regressions on Independent Slopes Model (PRISM) (Daly and others, 1997). No new calibration model runs were made to adjust any of the process-related parameters previously calibrated in the 2009 model.

Comparisons of Measured Hydrologic Data with Simulations by the 2009 and 2012 Models

Comparisons were made by running the model with the 2009 and 2012 parameter files and comparing selected simulated and measured variables for water years (WY) 2010 and 2011 (a water year starts on October 1 of the previous year and ends September 30 of the current year). Because the streamflow-gaging station Crab Creek at Irby, USGS station number 12465000, generally is the focus of interest for forecast runoff, this study compares simulated and measured runoff and other hydrologic variables in this part of the upper Crab Creek basin upstream of Irby (fig. 1).

The model does not simulate the peak discharges well for both water years, by under-simulating the WY 2010 peaks and over-simulating the WY 2011 peaks in Crab Creek (fig. 3). The runoff volumes are compared in table 1 for January 1 to June 30 (the runoff part of the year) and show under-simulation of runoff in five of the six comparisons and over-simulation in one comparison (Crab Creek at Irby in WY 2011). However, the differences between runoff simulated with the 2009 and 2012 models are small relative to the differences between the simulated and measured runoff. Runoff simulated with the 2012 model closely follows the pattern of runoff simulated with the 2009 model, but the 2012 model simulates slightly less runoff overall and a significant difference in the peak runoff in WY 2011 (the daily peak at Crab Creek at Irby simulated by the 2009 and 2012 models is 837 and 554 ft^3/s, respectively). The larger peak simulated by the 2009 model generally is due to the larger precipitation total (fig. 4A). Figure 4A shows a 2-year total of 29.60 in. for the 2009 model compared with 24.49 in. for the 2012 model for Hydrologic Response Unit (HRU, also known as MRU or Model Response Unit) 148, located near Davenport, Washington (fig. 2), and is representative of the highest annual precipitation in the study area. Soil moisture values for HRU 148 show similar patterns between the simulated values for the 2009 and 2012 models (fig. 4B), but both models miss some large variations indicated by the measured record. The measured soil moisture represents only the average of the 4- and 20-in. depths at one point in the watershed, whereas the simulated soil moisture represents the entire soil column averaged for a large area (9,976 acres for HRU 148); therefore, a close match between simulated and measured time series is not expected. However, the general pattern between simulated and measured soil moisture should be similar. The simulated soil moisture showed higher winter moisture values relative to the beginning moisture on September 1, 2009, than the measured moisture. However, the simulated soil moisture values returned to about the same initial September 2009 value in September 2010 and September 2011 whereas the measured September values in 2010 and 2011 were about 2 in. less than the September 2009 initial value.

The Continuous Frozen Ground Index (CFGI, fig. 4C) indicates when the ground is frozen or not. Molnau and Bissel (1983) originally developed the index and it use in the Potholes watershed model is described by Mastin (2009). The index increases when the daily air temperature is below 32°F. Increasing snow-cover depth tends to reduce the CFGI value and a user-defined parameter sets the daily decay of the CFGI value. After a user-defined threshold value is exceeded (137 in the Potholes watershed model), all simulated liquid water at the land surface of that HRU becomes surface runoff. By directing all the liquid water to the surface runoff outlet, the simulated runoff hydrograph becomes flashy and the peak discharges are much larger than they would be otherwise. The simulated CFGI time series for the 2009 and 2012 models shows a similar pattern for water years 2010 and 2011 for HRU

148 (fig. 4C), and generally increases as the measured soil temperature approaches and is below freezing. As soil temperatures increase, the CFGI values decrease. The CFGI never reached the CFGI threshold during these water years, so no large, flashy peaks are simulated (fig. 3).

It is apparent from the simulation of peak discharges in WYs 2010 and 2011 that the model cannot be relied on to accurately simulate peak discharges. This is consistent with the conclusions of Mastin (2009). Despite the poor performance in simulating peak discharges during the runoff season, the question remains whether the model can reasonably forecast seasonal runoff volumes, one of the primary uses of the model. The model has a forecast tool built into the programming of its Object User Interface (OUI; Markstrom and Koczot, 2008) that uses the Ensemble Streamflow Prediction (ESP) method (Day, 1985). ESP uses historical input data (beginning in WY 1950 for the Potholes models) to simulate an ensemble of possible runoff scenarios from the current point in time, and it orders the output by volume or peak discharge to create exceedance probabilities of the future runoff as a function of past climate (see Mastin [2009] for more detail). Generally, the 50-percent exceedance probability is considered the most likely runoff volume or peak discharge that can be expected to occur if model bias is ignored. To demonstrate the accuracy of the forecast tool, retrospective forecasts were made using the ESP method for the January 1 to June 30 runoff season for WYs 2010 and 2011 with input time series that ended on December 31, 2009, and December 31, 2010, respectively. The simulated 50-percent-exceedance-probability runoff volumes generated by the 2009 and 2012 models are shown in table 2 for each water year along with the measured data. Percent differences between the 50-percent-exceedance-probability runoff volume simulated by the 2012 model and the measured runoff volume are still high, with 5 of the 6 comparisons within 40 percent of the measured runoff volumes. One-half of the percent differences were within 17 percent of the measured runoff volumes and the extremes varied from -39.4 to 60.3 percent. These results are similar to the results of the comparisons between measured and simulated long-term mean monthly runoff values for January through June in the 2009 long-term model, which simulated three monthly runoff volumes less than 15 percent different from measured values and three monthly runoff volumes greater than 26 percent different from measured values (Mastin, 2009, table 9). Despite the poor fit between simulated and measured runoff, the model provides some useful volumetric runoff information within relatively large error bands.

New Real-Time Data-Retrieval Program, the Potholes Data Chimp

In addition to changes made to two meteorological data inputs to the model, the existing program to retrieve real-time data was revised completely and named the Potholes Data Chimp. The program, Potholes_Data_Chimp.exe, runs outside the model user interface, and must run prior to an ESP forecast to upload the latest data to the real-time data input file. Data specific to the Potholes watershed model are retrieved from several web sites and reformatted for model input (table 3). The first time the program is executed, it asks for the file name of the master data file. This file, called MasterDatafile.txt in the example in this report, contains data from October 1, 1949, to September 30, 2009, or later, formatted in the model input data format for daily precipitation, daily maximum temperature, and daily minimum temperature for the nine real-time meteorological stations (one row of data for each day). The Potholes Data Chimp appends new data to the master data file when the new data has a time stamp after the most recent existing data. Data with the same time stamp overwrites existing data, but the program will not overwrite data before October 1, 2009.

The data information window (fig. 5) appears upon startup of the Potholes Data Chimp. The start and end dates of the existing data file are provided in the Data File Information block, and the user enters the start and end dates of the desired retrieval of new data in the Enter Start and End Dates block. The program defaults to a start date of the day after the last date in the master data file and an end date of the current day. The user may enter other dates, but the program will not overwrite any data in the master file prior to October 1, 2009. After the desired dates have been entered, the user clicks the Start button to initiate the data retrieval. A progress bar shows the progress of the retrieval and a small pop-up window appears informing the user that the retrieval has been completed.

A recommended procedure is to locate the `Potholes_Data_Chimp.exe` file in the data directory along with the master data file. The data directory is located in the input directory, which is located in a directory path relative to the root directory (`oui_potholes`, fig. 6). The project directory `potholes` is located under the directory `oui_potholes` followed by the `mms_work/input/data` pathway showing the `Potholes_Data_Chimp.exe`, master data file (`MasterData.txt`), and the input data file used for ESP model runs (`pot_rt.data`).

After the data retrieval has been completed and the master data file has been updated, the user should delete the old `pot_rt.data` file and copy the updated master data file to a new `pot_rt.data` file. The model is then ready to run an ESP forecast.

Object User Interface for Making Watershed Model Runs and Viewing Data

The Object User Interface (OUI) is a computer application that manages the watershed model and associated temporal and spatial data to facilitate use of the model. The OUI has been configured specifically for the Potholes watershed model with a control file, project_potholes.xml, written in eXtensible Markup Language (XML). A more detailed discussion of the OUI can be found in the OUI user manual (Markstom and Koczot, 2008).

The OUI relies on model-input data, model-input variable, model-input parameter, spatial, and executable files maintained in a specific directory structure relative to the root directory named "oui_potholes" in the example shown in figure 6. The OUI files for the Potholes watershed model can be installed by extracting the files from the Win.zip file (potholes_model03_23_12.zip; file available from the author), which maintains the directory structure shown in figure 6. The OUI is written in Java and XML and it requires Java version 1.5.0_09 or later (accessed June 26, 2012, at *http://www.oracle.com/technetwork/java/javase/downloads/index.html*) to execute the program with a Windows operating system. To run the OUI, the user executes the oui_potholes.bat file in the oui_potholes/potholes directory by double-clicking the file name in the Windows Explorer program.

The OUI project file, project_potholes.xml, organizes the different spatial, model-input data, and executable elements of the project into a project tree structure. The elements are defined as tree nodes that are arranged in a hierarchical manner within a project tree that is visible to the user when opening the OUI window. Any tree node may contain other tree nodes similar to a file system on a computer where the root directory contains all the other directories and files (described in more detail by Markstrom and Kozat, 2008).

Major Tree Nodes

The following discussion about using the Potholes OUI program is arranged by the major tree nodes and their function in the order they appear in the opening window.

The three major tree nodes under the Potholes Project shown by the OUI include "Basin Maps," "Model Unit Maps," and "Models & Data." The nodes can be seen in the upper-left panel of the Potholes OUI window (fig. 7). Text in italics in this section refers to identical text in the OUI window pointing to various tree nodes and tree-node operations.

Basin Maps Major Tree Node

Tree nodes under the *Basin Maps* major tree node are selected by clicking the right button on the mouse (right-clicking) to display background GIS coverages without active data (active data can generate a process or a new screen when the GIS feature is clicked). A good starting point is to display the model units by right-clicking the *Models* node and then clicking the *Load* tab (not shown in fig. 7). This method works for all the themes. The selected theme will be "loaded" in the lower left panel of the OUI window called *Loaded Themes*. Clicking the *Visible* check box makes it visible in the right *Map Mode* panel of the OUI Window. Clicking the *Labels* check box adds labels to the map. The *Active* and *Query* check boxes do not do anything for this theme, and checking the *Attributes* check box will open a new window showing the attributes for this theme (the new window may be hidden behind the main OUI window). The following are the tree nodes under the *Basin Maps* major tree node that contain the shape files that are used to display spatial themes:

- *Lakes*   uses shape file: oui\potholes\oui\work\shapes\all_lakes.shp

- *Springs*   uses shape file: oui\potholes\oui\work\shapes\springs.shp

- *Streams*   uses shape file: oui\potholes\oui\work\shapes\all_str.shp

- *Models*   uses shape file: oui\potholes\oui\work\shapes\model_units.shp

- *Met-lt*   uses shape file: oui\potholes\oui\work\shapes\met_lt.shp

Model Unit Maps Major Tree Node

Tree nodes under the *Model Unit Maps* major tree node provide additional GIS coverages without active data. Load and display these themes in the same manner as described under "Basin Maps Major Tree Node" for the *Models* theme. Substitute "Crab Ck," "Lind," or "Rocky" for <model> as follows for a description of the contents of these tree nodes under the *Model Unit Maps* major tree node:

- *<model> model* Model unit subbasins

- *<model> MRUs* Model Response Units (MRUs) map for each model unit

- *DEM* digital elevation model display for each model unit

- *Slope* slope surfaces display computed from DEM for each model unit

- *Aspect* slope aspect display computed from DEM for each model unit

Models & Data Major Tree Node

The *Models & Data* major tree node is the main section for viewing input and output data and for running the models. All the tree nodes under this major tree node have additional tree nodes under them, which are described below.

Input Tree Node

The *Input* tree node is used to view the model input data. Tree node *MMS Data Files* (fig. 8) contains sub-nodes listed in the hierarchical bullets at the end of the "Input Tree Node" section. Time series plots can be made using station data for sites displayed by these sub-node themes. For example, a plot of precipitation at the Davenport station can be made by first loading the *Real-time Stations* theme (right-click the node *Real-time Stations* under the *Climate Data* node, then click the *Load* tab), and then click the *Visible*, *Labels*, *Active* and *Query* check boxes for the *Real-time Stations* theme in the *Loaded Themes* panel. A set of labeled box symbols will be visible in the *Map Mode* panel. Using the *Select* tool in the *Map Mode* panel, click the Davenport box (fig. 8). An informational pop-up box will appear, listing the three available variables (not shown). Select *precipitation* and a *Time Series Tool* window will appear (if the window is not visible, it may be hidden behind the main OUI window). Click *precip at Davenport* in the *Trace List* of the *Time Series Tool* window, click the drop-down menu item *Plots*, and select *Time Series*. A time series plot for all the available data will appear. Missing meteorological data are coded as -9999; therefore, the range of the y-axis may be large and make it difficult to view the real values ("-9" is used for missing discharge data). A box defining a zoom area can be drawn using the mouse to view the range you wish to see. Right-click in the plot for more options (fig. 8).

The hierarchical order of the tree nodes under the *Input* tree node follows the bulleted list below. These tree nodes allow the user to make graphs of climate data for real-time and long-term stations and of measured discharge using the method described above for precipitation at Davenport.

Input
- *MMS Data Files*
  - *Climate Data*
    - *Real-time Stations*
    - *Long-term Stations*
  - *Observed Runoff Data*
    - *Measured Discharge*

Single Run Tree Node

The *Single Run* tree node is used to make single runs for all three model units using user-supplied model run dates. Right-clicking on this node pops up a small *Run* button. Clicking on *Run* will cause the *Run MMS Model* window to appear. A user can enter the run dates and start the model run by clicking the *Run* button. Note that 1) 2 years should be run for the initial or "warm-up" period when the model is run, but the results are not used; 2) the long-term data file, which ends on September 30, 2004, is used as input; and 3) all three models run for the same period.

The sub-node *Single run Model Output* is used to plot the simulated discharge (variable segment_cfs) time series of selected locations of the last single model run. Right-clicking the sub-node displays the selected locations as point symbols in the *Map Mode* panel. After the *Active* and *Query* check boxes in the *Loaded Themes* panel are checked and a point location in the *Map Mode* panel is selected, a drop-down menu will appear with all the variables (flow-routing nodes on the stream network) from the last single model run that are available for plotting. For example, clicking the point symbol labeled "6" in the *Map Mode* will display a pop-up menu that asks *"Which variable for 6?"* and lists all the selected segment_cfs variables. Clicking the segment_cfs 6 in this pop-up menu will display the *Time Series Tool* window with *"segment_cfs 6 at 6"* in the *Trace List*. This plot is the simulated time series runoff for node 6 or Crab Creek at Irby. Appendix A provides a table and a map of the Potholes model flow-routing nodes, their identification numbers, and descriptions and locations of the stream-network points they represent (table A1 and fig. A1).

ESP Run Tree Node

The *ESP Run* tree node is used to make ESP model runs for all three models for the purpose of forecasting streamflows during a user-supplied forecast period. Right-clicking this node will display a small *Run* button. Clicking *Run* will cause a *Run MMS Model in ESP Mode* window to appear (fig. 9). This window allows a user to enter the forecast dates and then start an ESP model run by clicking the *Run* button. A model run is made beginning 2 years prior to the user-supplied forecast start date. (The 2 additional years serve to estimate initial antecedent conditions.) Each ESP run consists of a set of multiple model runs for the same period within the year, but uses different years of historical input data. The pot_rt.data file contains the historical input data for these model runs. Simulated results are saved in "statvar" files (files with "statvar" in the file name) in directory `../oui/potholes/mms_work/output/esp`. There is one output statvar file for each year of simulated runoff, such as `crab_ESP_1950.statvar`, which contains the output data for the ESP run for the Crab Creek Model Unit using WY 1950 input. The output statvar file lists the simulated runoff for all the selected routing nodes for each day in one row. The header of the file lists the order of the simulated discharge in each row by the segment_cfs index number.

Clicking sub-node *ESP Traces* will display a map with the location of streamflow routing nodes with ESP output in the *Map Mode* panel. Selecting one of these locations will open up the OUI *ESP Tool* window (fig. 9), which lists the available time series of simulated daily discharge for the selected location within the *Ensemble Traces* window. The listing includes one time series for each year of simulated runoff, and the time series ranked by volume, peak discharge, or year as selected by the user. Selecting one or more of these time series creates a composite hydrograph. Each plotted time series is a hydrograph referred to here as a "trace." The simulated 2-year-model-initiation hydrograph prior to the ESP period also is shown (the line labeled "init" in fig. 9). The user may right-click the graph for various zooming options, or may simply click and drag to define a zoom area. Functions under the Data Management Interface (DMI) drop-down menu are not operable at this time. By clicking drop-down menu *Reports* and *Write Report* (fig. 9), a summary report labeled *ESP Report* is generated that provides the runoff volume and peak discharge for each trace (year).

MMS Runs Tree Node

The *MMS Runs* tree node has three sub nodes, one for each model, that emulate the traditional Modular Modeling System (MMS, Leavesley and others, 1996) interface when activated. The interface allows users to adjust individual parameters and to make custom model runs. Right-clicking one of the three sub-nodes (labeled *Crab Creek MMS Model, Lind Coulee MMS Model,* and *Rocky Coulee MMS Model*) displays the *Run* button that will initiate the MMS user interface for the selected model (fig. 10). Clicking the drop-down *Run* menu in the opening window provides the option for making a single model run. Clicking this option displays a new window, the *MMS Run Control - Single Run* window (fig. 11). In this example, the model run start date is October 1, 2000, the end date is September 1, 2004, a variable file (crab.01.09.04) is being saved, the output statvar file is crab_swe_rt_statvar.dat, and one graph (*runtime graph*) that displays a user-selected variable time series while the model runs is being generated. The output *Statistics* file is checked, but this function currently is disabled in the OUI program. A variable file consists of variable values computed by the model for the end date of a model run.

Additional background information about the Potholes watershed model and its OUI is provided in Appendix A.

Method for Collecting Snow Data and Incorporating the Data into the Watershed Model

The watershed model simulates the density, depth, and snow-water equivalent (SWE) of snow on each HRU created for the model. However, the simulation of the current snowpack in the basin may be in error at the time the user wishes to make a runoff prediction. In order to check the accuracy of the model or to update the model with measured data, the actual snowpack in the basin can be estimated from readings at snow courses. Currently (2012), there are no snow pillows or weather stations in the basin that measure snow density or SWE. This section of the report describes a procedure for making measurements on an existing network of snow courses using a snow-measuring kit such as the Snowmetrics™ kit (Snowmetrics, 2012), converting the point measurements to a spatial estimate of snowpack in the basin, and incorporating the spatial estimate in the watershed model.

Measurements of Snow

The goal of the snow survey is to measure snow depth and snow density and to combine the two measurements to estimate SWE for the current snowpack in the Potholes Reservoir basin. Data measured at nine snow-course locations in or near the basin have been used previously to estimate the spatial extent of the three snow variables throughout the basin, and the snow-course locations continue to be the suggested sites for further snow surveys (fig. 12). After the spatial extent of the snow variables has been estimated, the data can be used to update the current snowpack conditions simulated by the watershed model to try to improve forecasts of runoff volumes. This type of "direct-insertion" approach has not always been successful in improving runoff forecasts. Clark and others (2006) provide a good review of various techniques that have been used to assimilate snow-covered area or SWE information into watershed models. As an example, figure 13 shows the SWE measured at nine locations in January 2004 and estimated values throughout the model domain. In this example, the data were entered into a GIS and, using an inverse-distance-weighted (IDW) interpolation method, the SWEs measured at the nine point locations were distributed throughout the model domain as gridded values. The gridded values were then assigned to HRUs in the watershed models to replace simulated SWE values.

The nine locations of the snow-survey sites are documented in Appendix B of this report.

Snow-Survey Methodology

The general method used to make a snow survey at a site in the study area has been adapted from a method by the U.S. Department of Agriculture (1984). The idea of a set snow course that generally has about 10 sample points along a line is retained, but the use of snow sampling tubes is not recommended because the snow generally is too shallow in the study area for accurate sampling with a snow tube. Instead of using snow tubes to sample the snow, a cutter or small tool (often used by avalanche forecasters to sample snow layers in a snow pit for snow density) is described in the following section as the recommended tool to sample the snow. The general method is:

1) **Measure the snow depth**. Use the folding ruler or tape measure to measure the snow depth at 10 equally spaced locations along a snow course that is documented in the site location maps in Appendix B. The snow course should be undisturbed and without drifts. In the snow course descriptions (Appendix B), the snow courses were generally 135-ft long and depths were measured every 15 ft beginning at the start of the snow course. Preferably, a cloth tape is placed along the course, but a well-defined pace by the surveyor also can be used.

2) **Measure the snow density**. At two to four sites along the snow course, snow pits are dug and one or more snow samples are retrieved from each pit and measured for snow density. In the Crab Creek basin, the snow usually is not deep and a pit is dug simply with one swipe of a shovel. If distinct layers can be seen in the snow pit, a density sample is needed from each layer and the layer depth range needs to be recorded. At each layer where a density sample is collected, the SWE is calculated, averaged for the profile, and then averaged again with other profile densities for the snow course. The text in italics is from Snowmetrics (2012) and describes how to sample a snow pit:

Dig snow pit wall or surface to be sampled. Shave the wall or surface with a flat-bladed shovel to give a smooth sampling surface. Surface must not be rough or sampling error will result. Position cutter perpendicular to surface in both vertical and horizontal directions.

Insert cutter at desired location. Be sure to insert cutter perpendicular to the surface so that the entire back of the cutter is flush with the snow surface when the cutter is all the way in. Do not attempt to straighten cutter after it is partially inserted or sampling error will result. It is better to move cutter and resample correctly. Do not push cutter in farther than snow surface or over sampling will occur. [It may be preferable to have a little snow come out the end of the cutter to ensure a full sample (E. Josberger, U.s. Geological Survey, oral commun., 2011)]

Place lid adjacent to top edge of cutter at an angle close to the angle of the upper cutter surface.

Hold cutter in place with one hand while inserting cutter lid in with the other. Do not allow cutter to slide back as lid is pressed in as undersampling will occur.

In consolidated or wet snow, once the lid is pressed in and the sample has been isolated, the cutter and sample may be removed and weighted while the lid is left in. In new, unconsolidated, weak, or kinetic (depth hoar) snow, the lid should be removed from the pit wall with the cutter to insure no sample loss.

Transfer the snow sample to the plastic baggie hanging from your spring scale. The weight in grams is simply multiplied by 4 to get density in kilograms per meter cubed (kg m -3), because the sample size is 250 cc. For example: a weight in grams of 90 gives 90 x 4 = 360 kg m-3. Percent density is calculated by dividing the number above by 1000 (36%). If you are using a digital top-loading scale, the lid is removed after the sample is turned upright, and the sample (still in the cutter) is placed directly on the scale.

Best results are obtained by inserting the flat bottom of the cutter vertically into the snowpack because this insures that heterogeneous layers are sampled evenly by the wedge shaped cutter. Hold the cutter handle in your left hand as you would a key being inserted into a lock; and hold the lid in your right hand. Reverse this procedure if you are left handed. Since the lid perturbs the snow above and below the cutter, a continuous density should be sampled by staggering alternate samples to one side or the other.

3) **Collect miscellaneous data**. The Snowmetrics™ kit includes a stem thermometer, a magnifying glass, and a millimeter grid for snow crystal measurements. Use the stem thermometer to collect air temperature, snow temperature for each layer at which a snow-density sample is collected, and soil temperature. Using the magnifying glass and millimeter grid, sprinkle a few snow grains under the magnifying glass to determine the shape and size of the snow crystals. Note the roundness or sharpness of the crystals and the shape—needle-like, prismatic, plate-like, star-like, and so on. Record the snow crystal data in the Remarks section of the field sheet. See the proposed field sheet layout (fig. 14).

Distributing Snow-Course Information throughout the Watershed

After point measurements of snow density and SWE have been made, the variables need to be estimated throughout the watershed model domain. The color-shaded information shown in figure 13 illustrates how the point measurements of SWE have been distributed throughout the Potholes Reservoir basin using an IDW interpolation method.

The procedure to distribute the snow-course data to the watershed is best described by an example. The following example creates a grid of SWE values for the January 3-4, 2004, data for the basin using Arc and Grid commands for the Environmental Systems Research Institute ArcInfo® GIS in ArcInfo Workstation mode using an existing grid of the study area boundary (sa) and a grid of watershed model HRUs.

1) The following is from an ASCII file (called sno_crs_pts.txt) of the point IDs, the X and Y coordinates for the snow course locations (UTM zone 11, datum NAD 83, units = meters) and the measured SWE (inches). This same file can be used in future snow surveys by updating the fourth column of data with current SWE values. Table 4 relates the point identifiers in this file to the snow courses.

```
        1    0.3094002E+06    0.5242992E+07  1.06
        2    0.3271944E+06    0.5276113E+07  1.26
        3    0.3428339E+06    0.5283372E+07  4.14
        4    0.3730221E+06    0.5290695E+07  5.10
        5    0.4149700E+06    0.5278735E+07  5.18
        6    0.4058188E+06    0.5258474E+07  4.28
        7    0.3943122E+06    0.5219253E+07  4.01
        8    0.3580135E+06    0.5240782E+07  3.56
        9    0.3413762E+06    0.5211914E+07  3.29
END
```

2) Using the IDW grid command, the text file "sno_crs_pts.txt," and an existing study area boundary grid, sa, the grid of SWE, swe_jan04_sa, was generated. The following three commands at the GRID level were used:
   Grid: setwindow sa
   Grid: swe_jan04 = IDW (sno_crs_pts.txt, #, #, 2, sample, 9, 50000, 90)
   Grid: jan04_sa = con(sa > 0, swe_jan04)

The jan04_sa grid now can be plotted to show the distribution of SWE from the nine discrete points in the basin to the entire basin.

Grid: gridp jan04_sa

Adding Distributed Snow Information to the Current Watershed Model

Prior to adding the current condition of SWE to the watershed model, it should be determined whether conditions are meaningfully different from the simulated SWE, and thus whether the simulated SWE values need to be replaced. In the description that follows, steps 1 through 4 compute the upper Crab Creek basin SWE volume for the simulated and measured estimates. Steps 5 and 6 outline how a forecast model run using the ESP method can be made using the measured SWE values.

1) Using the "combine" and "zonalmean" grid commands, create a new grid that merges SWE data with an existing HRU grid for the Crab Creek modeling unit (crab_hru):

   *Grid: out_jan04 = combine(crab_hru, zonalmean(crab_hru, (jan04_sa * 100)))*

   NOTE: The 100 multiplier converts the SWE values expressed in fractions of inches (real number) to hundreds of inches (an integer) so that an attribute table can be generated (grid attribute tables only contain integers).

2) Create a text file of SWE values ordered by HRU number.

   The grid attribute data should look like this:

   Grid: list out_jan04.vat

Record	VALUE	COUNT	CRAB_HRU	XYXY027
1	1	8280	11	458
2	2	5077	50	500
3	3	1248	12	485
4	4	2825	15	503
.	.	.	.	.
.	.	.	.	.
.	.	.	.	.

   Write the HRU and SWE data to a file, swe_jan04.txt:

   Grid: listoutput swe_jan04.txt

   Grid: list out_jan04.vat CRAB_HRU XYXY027

   Grid: listoutput screen   [return output to the screen]

3) Import the text file (swe_jan04.txt) into a spreadsheet (table 5). Sort the SWE values of the last column of the text file by HRU number and convert values of hundreds of inches of SWE to inches of SWE. In the spreadsheet, the area in acres for each HRU (parameter hru_area in the parameter file of the model) has been imported and sorted by HRU number. Finally, the volume of SWE by HRU (table 5) and total SWE volume for the modeling unit can be computed in acre-feet and mean depth in inches.

4) Compute the model-simulated basin SWE for the Crab Creek Modeling Unit and compare the results with measured snow-survey data.

   a) In the oui_potholes/potholes directory, click the file crab_swe_rt.bat to start the model
   b) Click the *Run* drop-down menu and *Single Run.*
   c) Enter the *Model End Date* as the date of the snow survey, and enter a start date of September 1 that is 3-4 years prior to the snow survey date (fig. 11).

d) Check the *Variable Save:* check box and enter a file name for the variable file (fig. 11). The example uses the file name "crab.01.09.04" because this file will save all the variables on the end date of January 9, 2004. This file can be updated later with measured SWE data to make a forecast ESP model run.

e) Click the *Start* button (fig. 11) to run the model.

f) After the model has ended, exit the program, and open file crab_swe_rt_statvar.dat in the oui_potholes/potholes/mms_work/output directory. Read the last value for the snow survey date. This is the mean depth of the simulated SWE in inches for the Crab Creek Modeling Unit.

g) Compare the snow-survey-derived mean depth with the simulated mean depth. In this example, the snow-survey-derived mean depth was 3.93 in. (about 5 times the simulated mean depth of 0.744 in.).

5) Edit the variable file if the simulated and measured SWE values are determined to be substantially different. If the measured SWE for the basin is much different from the simulated basin-wide SWE, as is evident in our example for January 2004, the measured snow-survey data can be used to update the variable file. These data will modify the simulated current conditions prior to making an ESP model run to forecast seasonal runoff volumes for the upper Crab Creek basin. This step begins the process of editing the variable file, crab.01.09.04, created in the last step. Four snow-related variables will be edited in the variable file: (1) SWE, in inches (pkwater_equiv); (2) free water in the snowpack, in inches (freeH20), computed as 2 percent of the SWE when the snowpack temperature is $0^{\circ}C$; (3) snowpack ice (pk_ice), computed as SWE minus free water; and (4) snowpack depth (pk_depth), computed as SWE divided by snowpack density. The variable file is an ASCII file that consists of one long column of data ordered by HRU number (1-387, in the case of the Crab Creek model) with sets of data separated by a line with "####," a line with the variable name, and four lines of header information.

a) Begin by creating another sheet in the spreadsheet file created in step 3 and copying the SWE data sorted by HRU to the new sheet. If not done already, convert the units of the SWE data to inches.

b) Open the variable file in directory oui_potholes/potholes/mms_work/input/vars (crab.01.09.04, in this example) in a text editor, search for "pk_temp" (snowpack temperature), select the data beginning five lines after "pk_temp," and copy the data to the new sheet in the spreadsheet file. Be careful to align the data so that the SWE data for an HRU is aligned by row with the pk_temp data for the same HRU.

c) Calculate values for freeh2o for each HRU in a new spreadsheet as 2 percent of pkwater_equiv if the pk_temp is 0.0. If pk_temp is not 0.0, the freeh2o value is 0 (if the pkwater_equiv data is in column C and the pk_temp data is in column E, then the formula for freeh2o in row 5 is "=IF(E5=0, C5*0.02, 0)" (fig. 15).

d) Create a column for pk_ice that is equal to pkwater_equiv minus freeh2o (fig. 15).

e) Create a column for pk_depth that is equal to pk_water divided by density. The density is available from the snow survey (average = 0.204 in decimal percent for this example). Note that the density is not used in the calculations of runoff; therefore, it is not critical to assign an exact value to density.

f) Replace the existing data in the variable file with new variable data for pkwater_equiv, freeh2o, pk_ice, and pk_depth. Be sure that all data in the spreadsheet are left justified. Update one variable at a time by first searching for the variable name in the variable file, copy the data from the spreadsheet, paste the data in the variable file beginning five rows below the variable name, and delete the old data for that variable.

6) Make an ESP run with the updated variable file.

The ESP function in the OUI does not use the variable file for generating the individual traces as it did in earlier versions of the OUI. Instead, a Perl script for Windows has been developed to make an ESP model run using the variable file created in step 5 called crab.01.09.04.txt in this example. (NOTE: ActivePerl for Windows is needed to run the script; it can be downloaded at no cost from the following web site, accessed June 26, 2012, at *http://www.activestate.com/activeperl/downloads/thank-you?dl=http://downloads.activestate.com/ActivePerl/releases/5.14.2.1402/ActivePerl-5.14.2.1402-MSWin32-x86-295342.msi*)

Prior to running the Perl script, it is important to make an ESP model run using the OUI for the same ESP start and end dates as will be used in the script. The Perl script will substitute the new data for the same period after the warm-up period in the original OUI-generated ESP files.

In the directory oui_potholes/potholes, run the script called "crab_updated_swe_rt.pl" by double-clicking the file name in Windows Explorer. The opening screen for the script will appear (fig. 16). In this example, a start date of January 10, 2004, and an end date of April 30, 2004, are used with the edited variable file crab.01.09.04.txt. The script runs the ESP model for the Crab Creek Model Unit and saves the output traces in a file name different than the output traces made running ESP with the OUI. After the script has run, the user can restart the OUI, display the ESP report (fig. 9) and generate new forecasts. The new forecasts are based on the measured snow-survey-derived data that replace the simulated current conditions of the snowpack for the Crab Creek Model Unit.

Summary

The U.S. Geological Survey (USGS) and the Bureau of Reclamation (Reclamation) have maintained a collaborative relationship in the development of watershed models for the drainage basins to Potholes Reservoir, Washington, which is managed by Reclamation along with a canal system to irrigate thousands of acres in the Columbia Basin Project. A previous USGS Scientific Investigations Report documents the development of a watershed model (2009 model) for these drainage basins. Since 2009, two new meteorological sites with real-time telemetry have been established in and near the study area. Adding these sites to the model required some updates to the model (2012 model) and the development of a new real-time data retrieval system. Model runs with the 2009 model and the 2012 model show similar results, and comparisons with measured data confirm the conclusions in the previous report that the model is not reliable in simulating runoff from individual storms, but has been successful in forecasting runoff volumes over a season. Updates to the model were made and a new real-time retrieval program called the Potholes Data Chimp was created; both are described in this report. A method of collecting snow data at nine historical measurement locations is described along with a method of incorporating the data into forecast model runs.

References Cited

Bureau of Reclamation, 2012a, AgriMet--The Pacific Northwest Cooperative Agricultural Weather Network: Bureau of Reclamation database, accessed May 14, 2012, at *http://www.usbr.gov/pn/agrimet/*.

Bureau of Reclamation, 2012b, Hydromet: Bureau of Reclamation database, accessed May 14, 2012, at *http://www.usbr.gov/pn/hydromet/*.

Clark, M.P., Slater, A.G., Barrett, A.P., Hay, L.E., McCabe, G.J., Rajogopalan, B. and Leavesley, G.H., 2006, Assimilation of snow covered area information into hydrologic and land-surface models, Advances in Water Resources, v29, p. 1209-1221.

Daly, Christopher, Taylor, George, and Gibson, Wayne, 1997, The PRISM approach to mapping precipitation and temperature: Proceeding of the 10th Conference on Applied Climatology, Reno, Nevada, American Meteorological Society, p. 10-12, accessed October 2011 at *http://www.prism.oregonstate.edu/pub/prism/docs/appclim97-prismapproach-daly.html*.

Day, G.N., 1985, Extended streamflow forecasting using NWSRFS: American Society of Civil Engineers, Journal of Water Resources Planning and Management, v. 111, no.2, p.157—170.

Leavesley, G.H., Lichty, R.W., Troutman, B.M., and Saindon, L.G., 1983, Precipitation-runoff modeling system—User's manual: U.S. Geological Survey Water-Resources Investigation Report 83-4238, 207 p.

Leavesley, G.L., Restrepo, P.J., Markstrom, S.L., Dixon, Mike, and Stannard, L.G., 1996, The Modular Modeling System (MMS) user's manual: U.S. Geological Survey Open-File Report 96-151, 175 p.

Markstrom, S.L., and Koczot, K.M., 2008, User's manual for the object user interface (OUI)—An environmental resource modeling framework: U.S. Geological Survey Open-File Report 2008-1120, 39 p.

Mastin, M.C., 2009 Watershed models for decision support for inflows to Potholes Reservoir, Washington: U.S. Geological Survey Scientific Investigations Report 2009-5081, 54 p.

Molnau, M., and Bissel, 1983, A continuous frozen ground index for flood forecasting: Vancouver, Wash., Proceedings of the 51st Annual Meeting of the Western Snow Conference, p. 109-119.

Snowmetrics, 2012, Tools for avalanche forecasting and snow research: Snowmetrics Web site, accessed August 13, 2012, at *http//www.snowmetrics.com/store/*.

U.S. Department of Agriculture, 1984, Snow survey sampling guide: Soil Conservation Service Agricultural Handbook Number 169, 32 p.

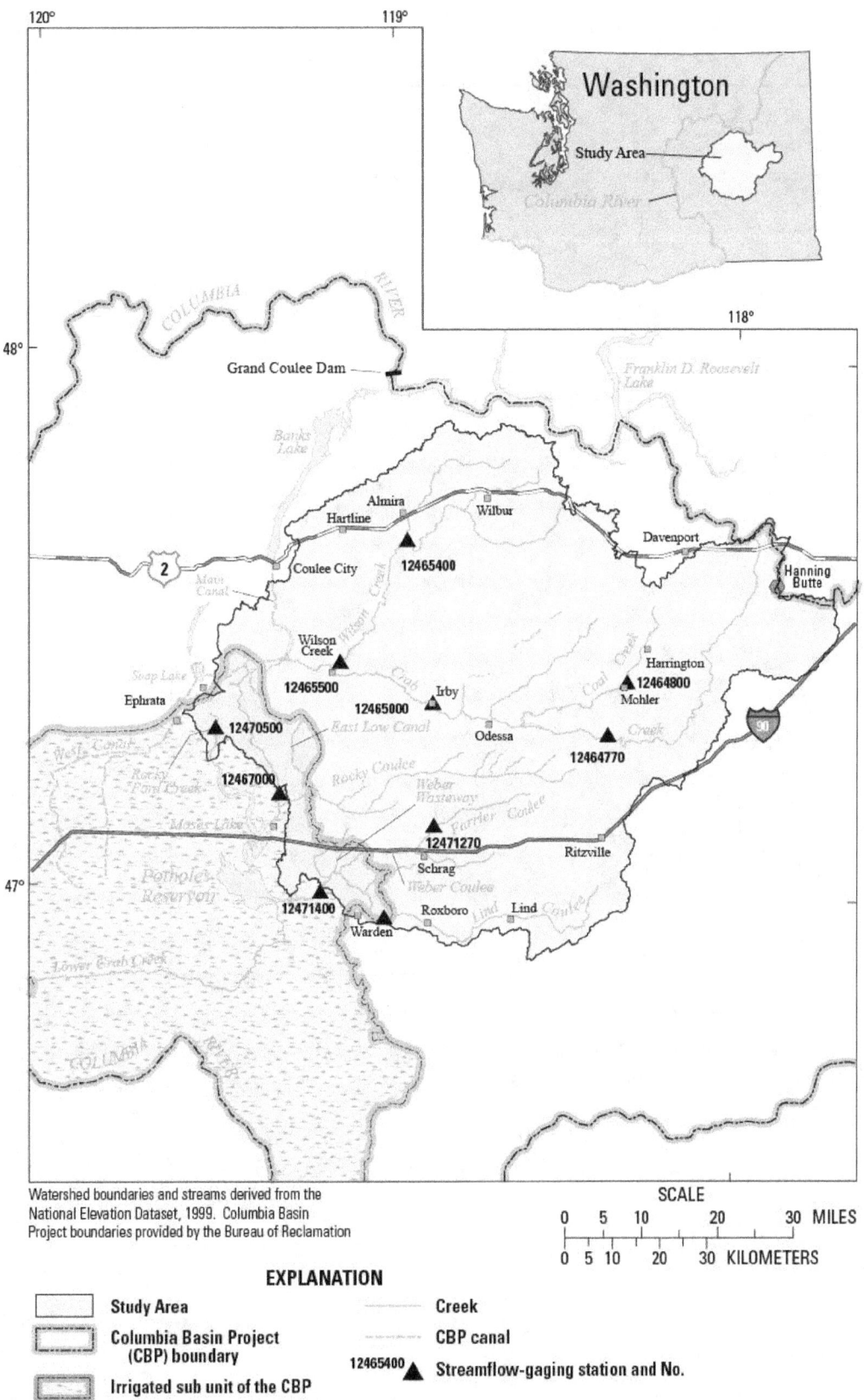

Figure 1. Locations of streamflow-gaging stations and boundaries of the Columbia Basin Project and study area in the Potholes Reservoir basin, Washington.

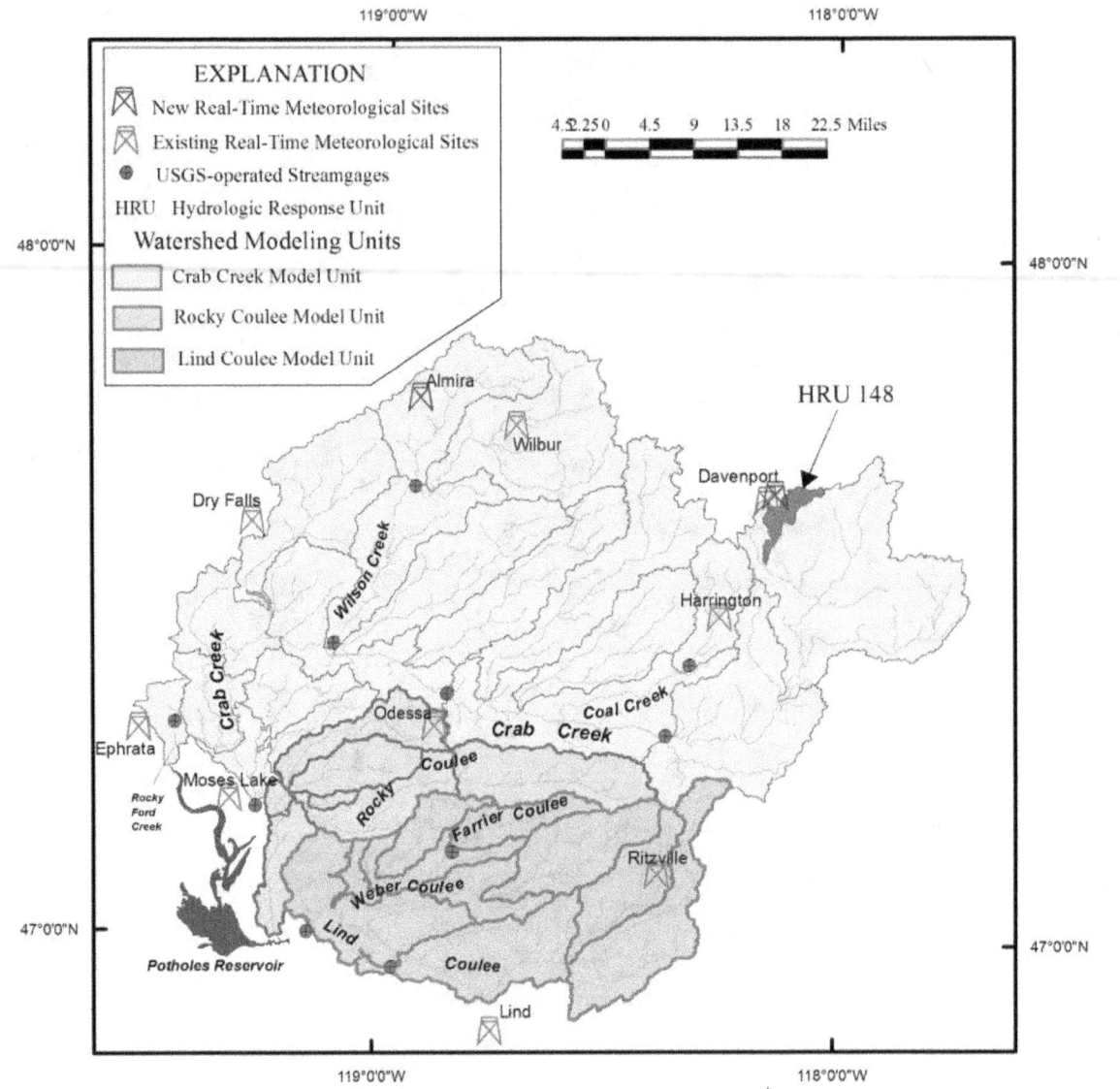

Figure 2. Watershed modeling units, streamflow-gaging stations and new and existing meteorological sites that provide input data to the watershed models, Potholes Reservoir basin, Washington.

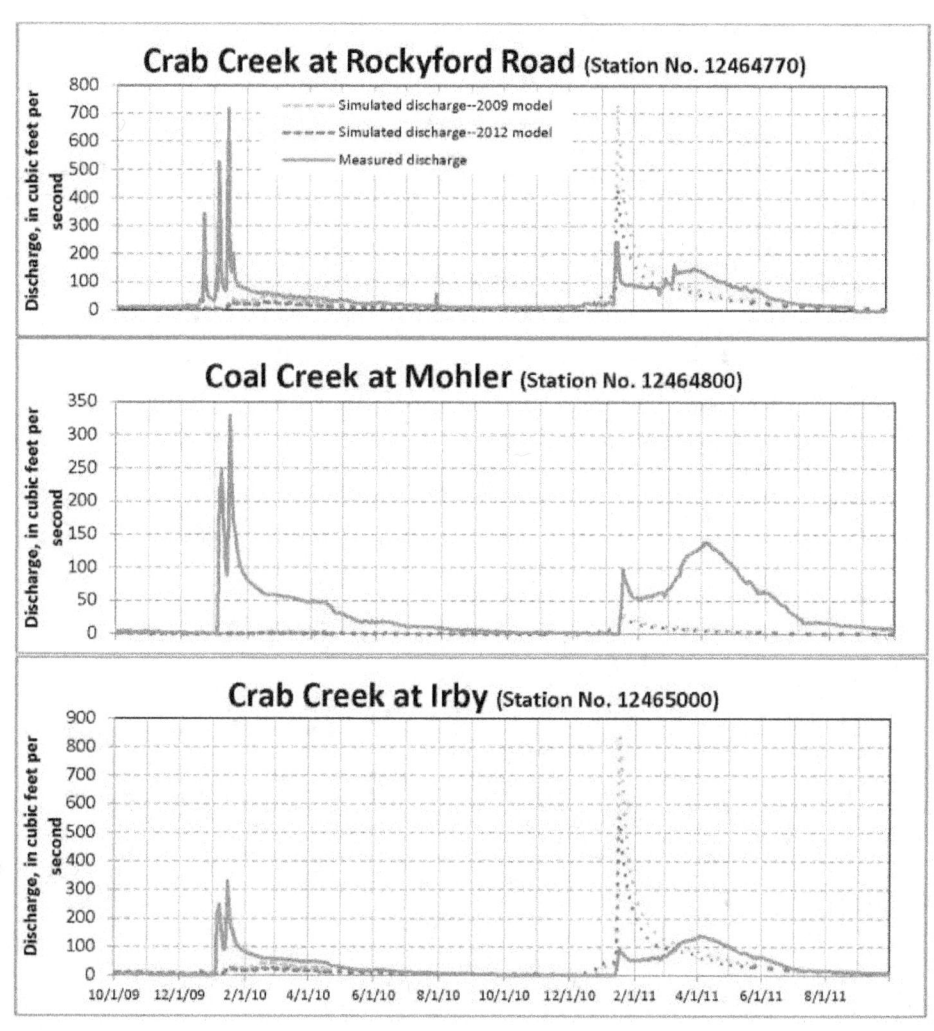

Figure 3. Comparison of measured discharge and discharge simulated with the 2009 and 2012 models at three streamflow-gaging stations, upper Crab Creek basin, Washington water years 2010-11.

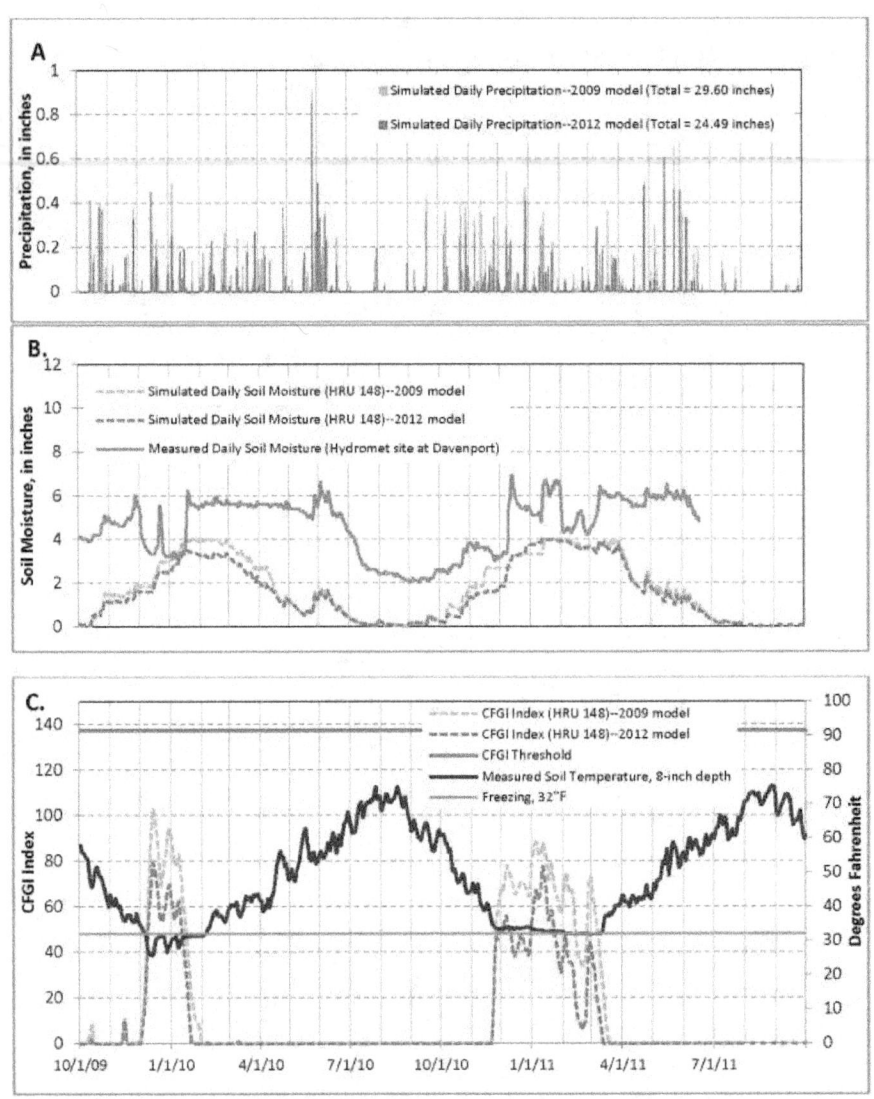

Figure 4. Measured hydrologic variables and hydrologic variables simulated using the 2009 and 2012 models at Hydrologic Response Unit (HRU) 148 near Davenport, Washington, water years 2010-11. (A) Simulated daily precipitation, (B) simulated daily soil moisture and measured soil moisture at Davenport (measured soil moisture is the average of the soil moisture at 4 and 20 in. depths); and (C) Continuous Frozen Ground Index (CFGI) and measured soil temperature at Davenport.

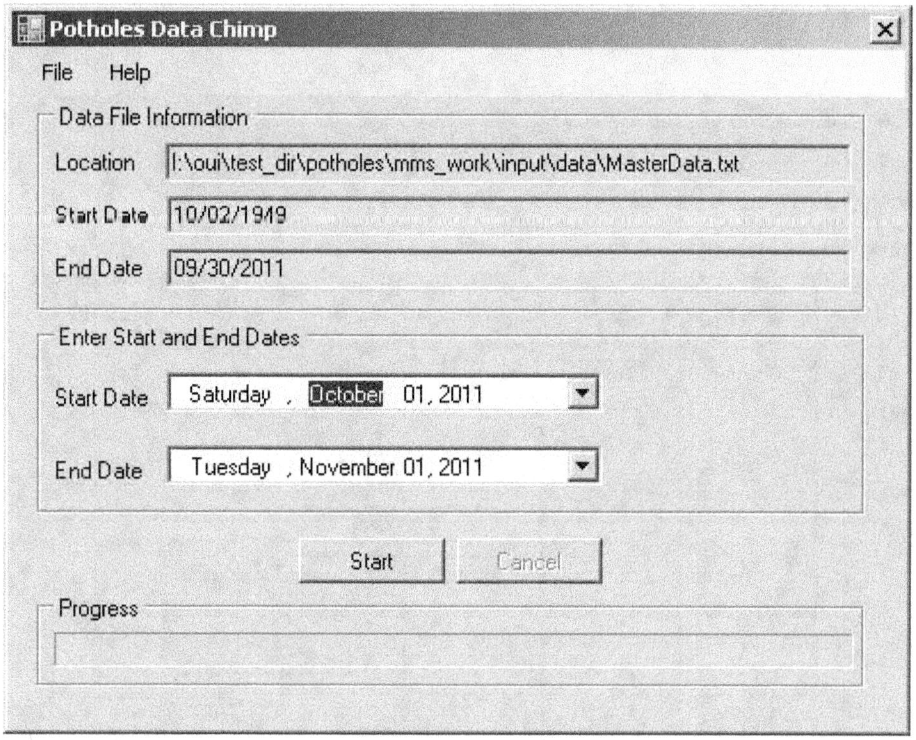

Figure 5. Screen capture showing the Potholes Data Chimp data information window.

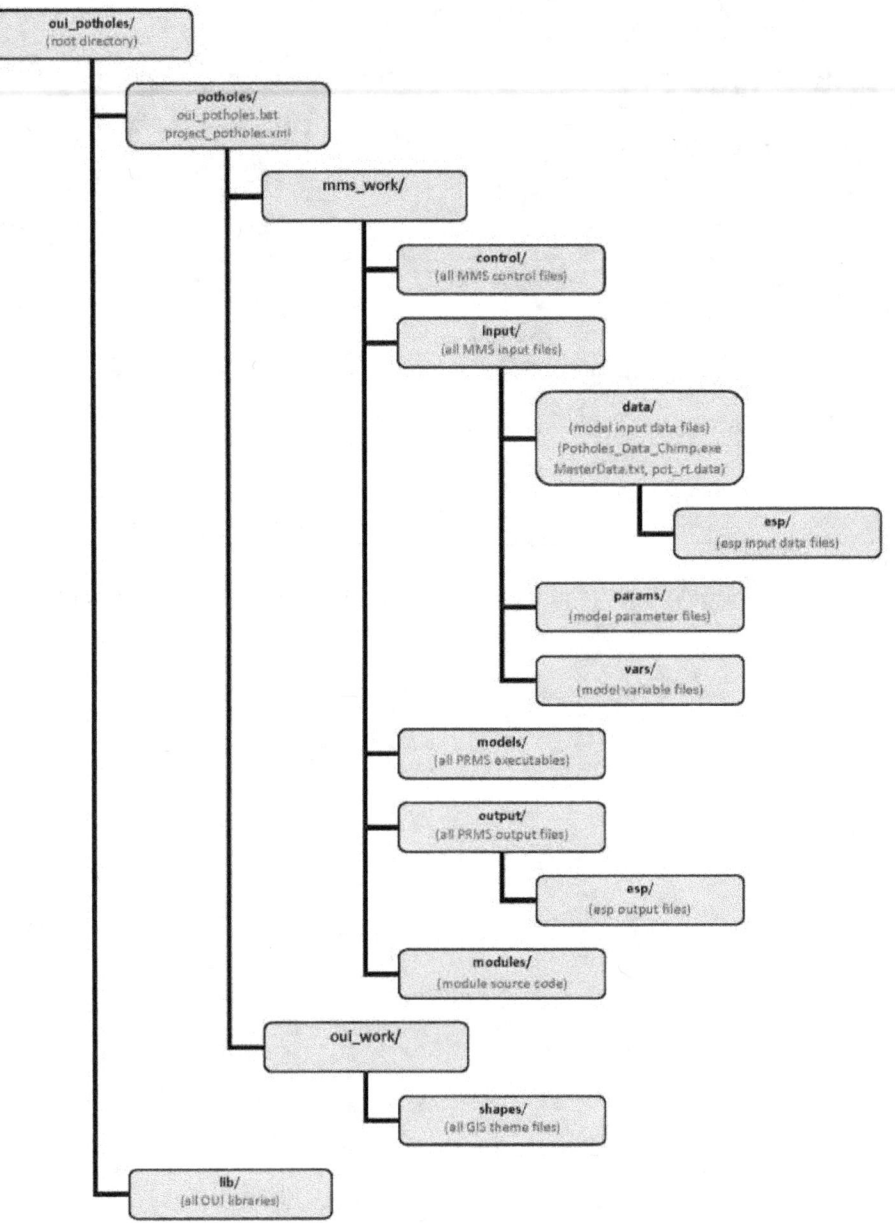

Figure 6. Object User Interface (OUI) directory structure for the Potholes watershed model, Potholes Reservoir basin, Washington. [MMS, Modular Modeling System; esp, ensemble streamflow prediction; PRMS, Precipitation Runoff Modeling System; GIS, Geographic Information System]

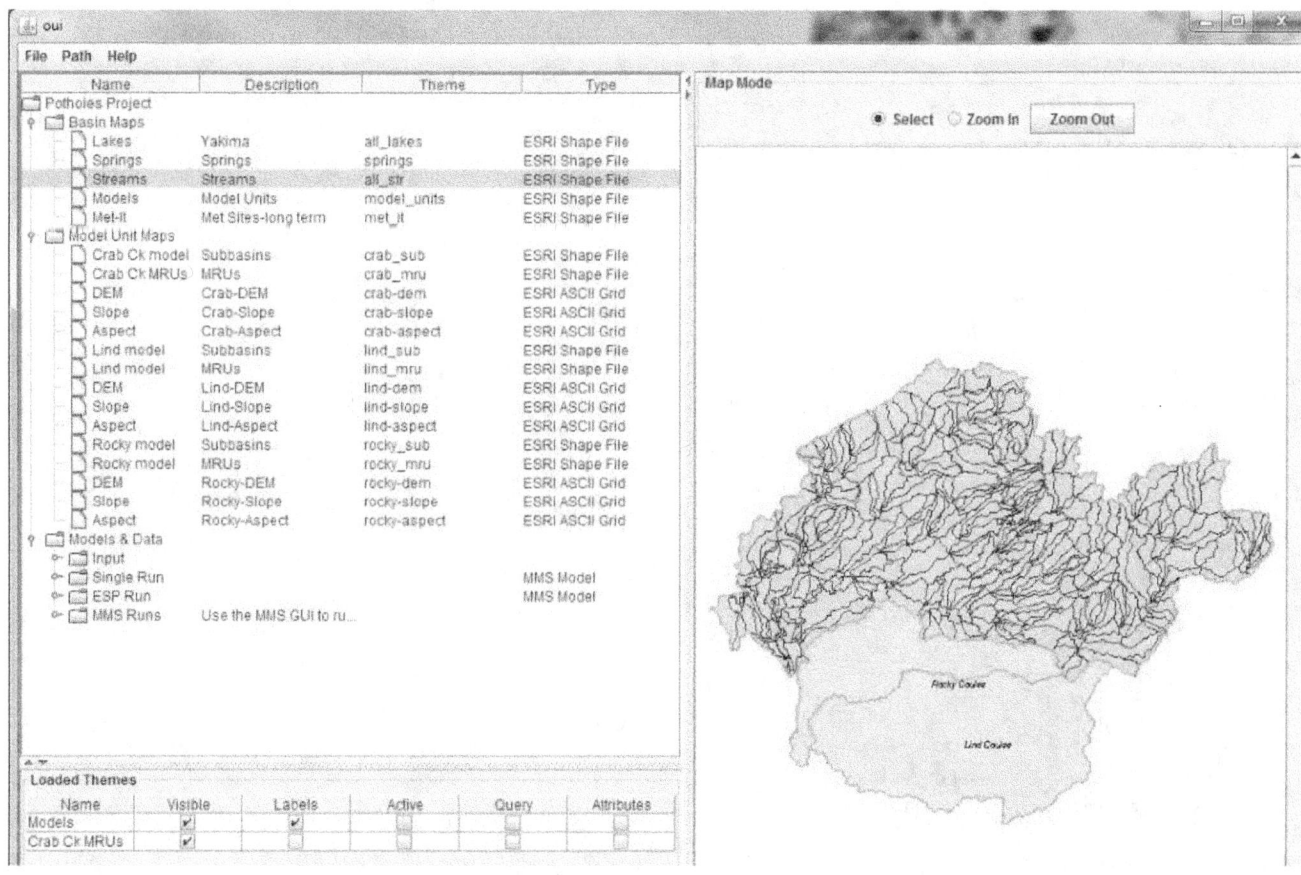

Figure 7. Screen shot of the Object User Interface (OUI) opening screen showing the tree nodes under the three major tree nodes (left panel) and the Map Mode panel (right panel) showing maps of two selected tree node elements, "Models" and "Crab Ck MRUs" from the "Model Unit Maps" tree node.

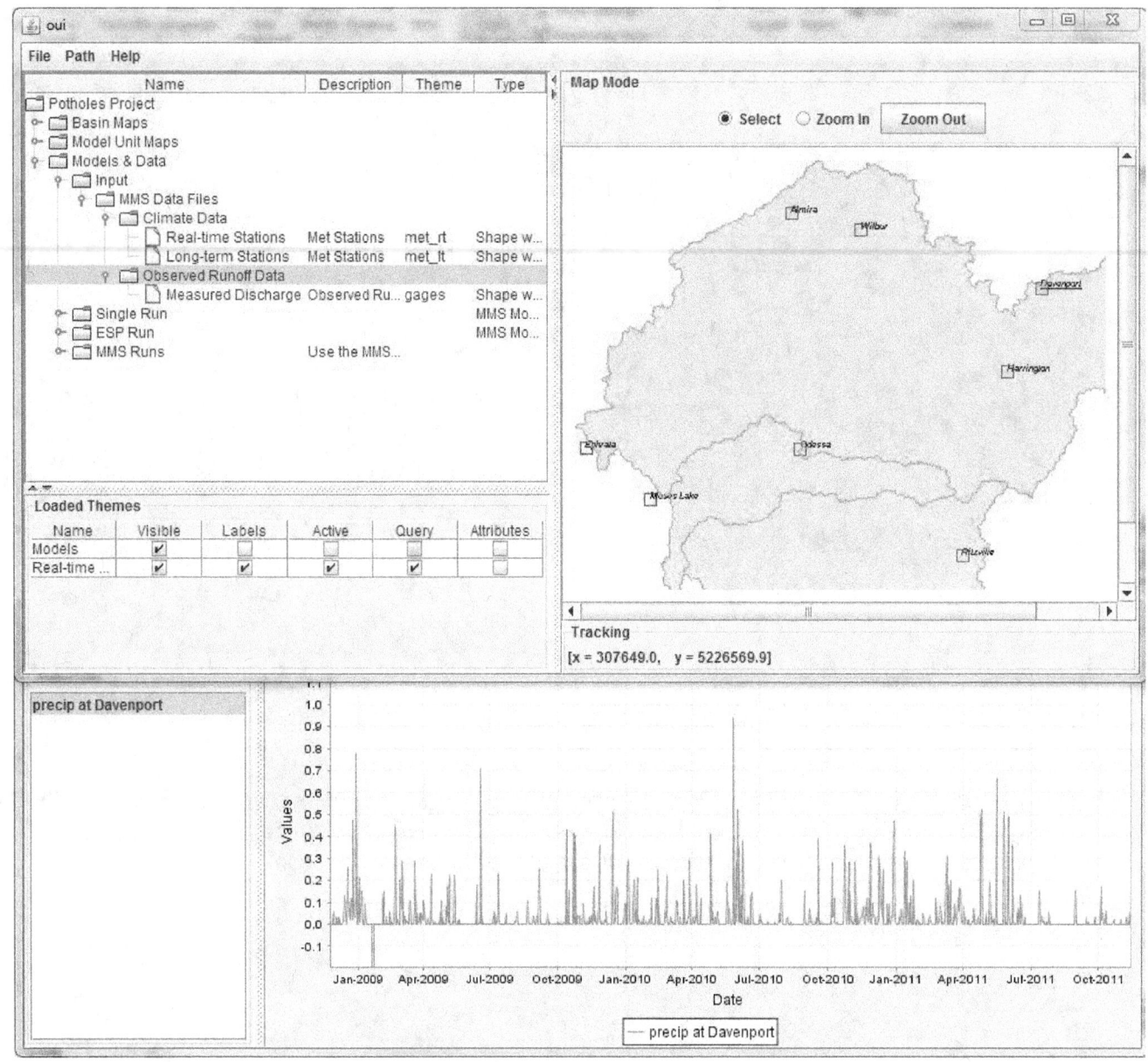

Figure 8. Screen shot of the Object User Interface (OUI) main window showing the real-time stations in the Map Mode window with the Davenport, Washington, station selected (top), and the Time Series Tool window with a zoomed-in plot of precipitation input data.

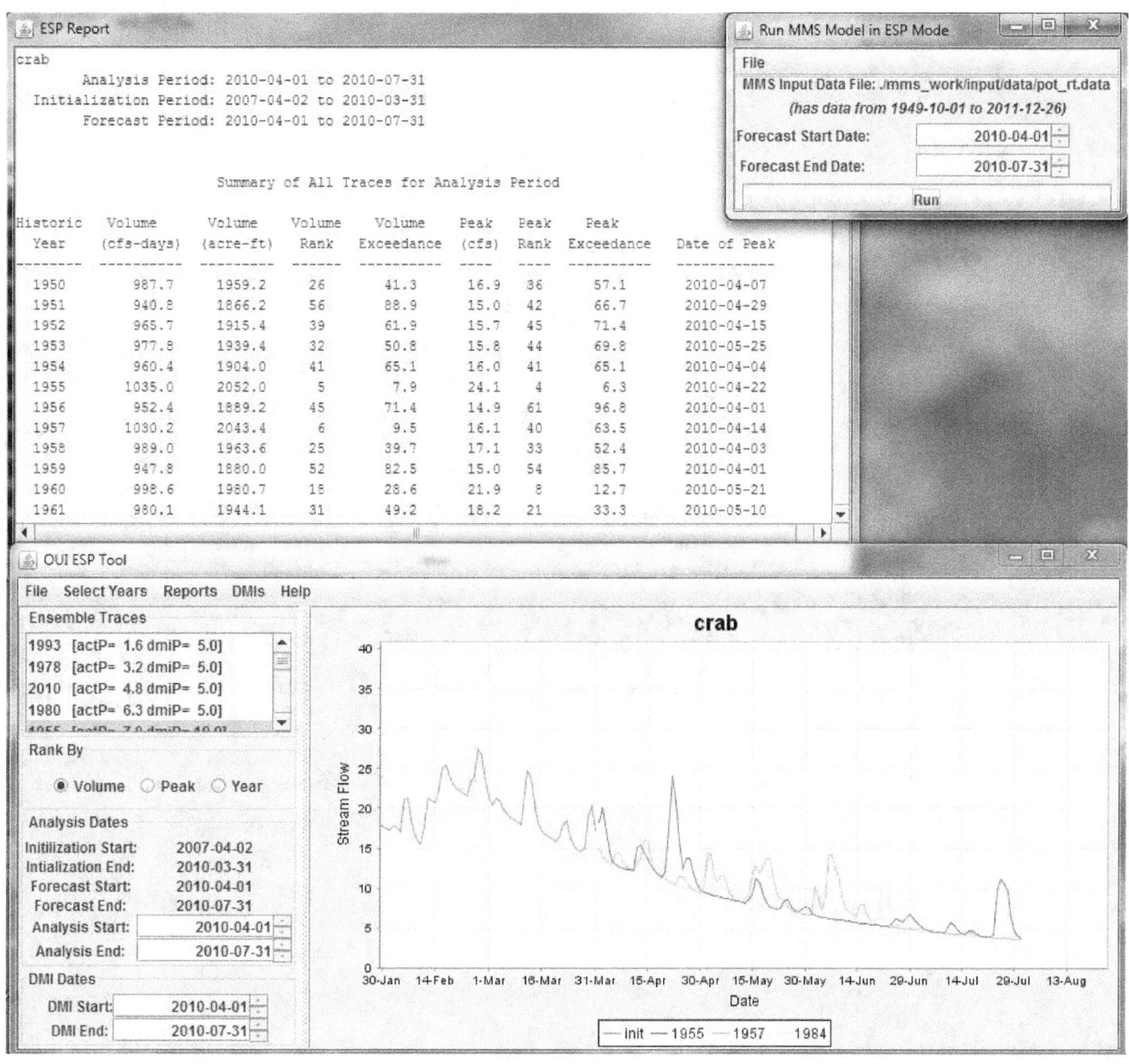

Figure 9. Screen capture of the ESP report, Run MMS Model in ESP Mode, and OUI ESP Tool windows.

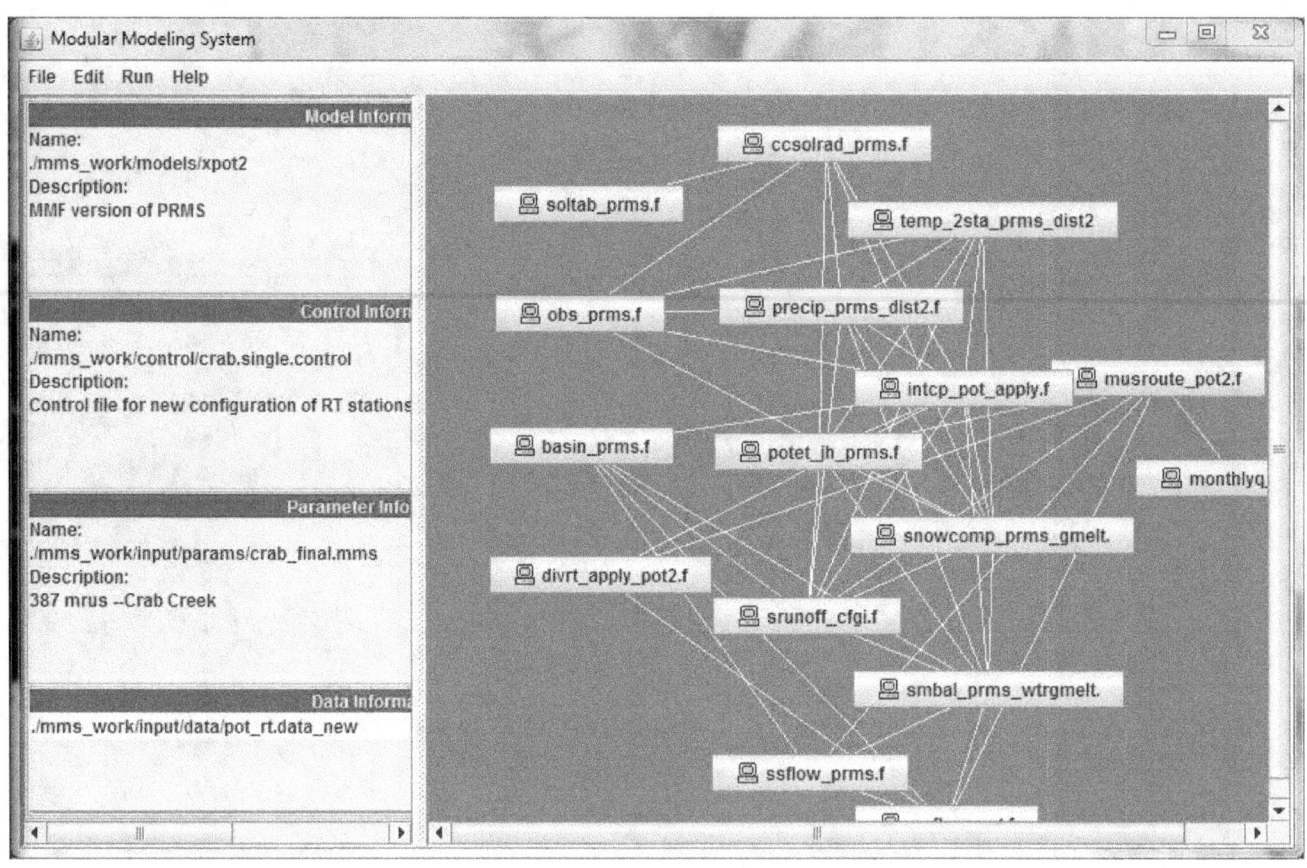

Figure 10. Screen capture of the opening window for the Modular Modeling System (MMS) traditional user interface for the Crab Creek model, Potholes Reservoir basin, Washington.

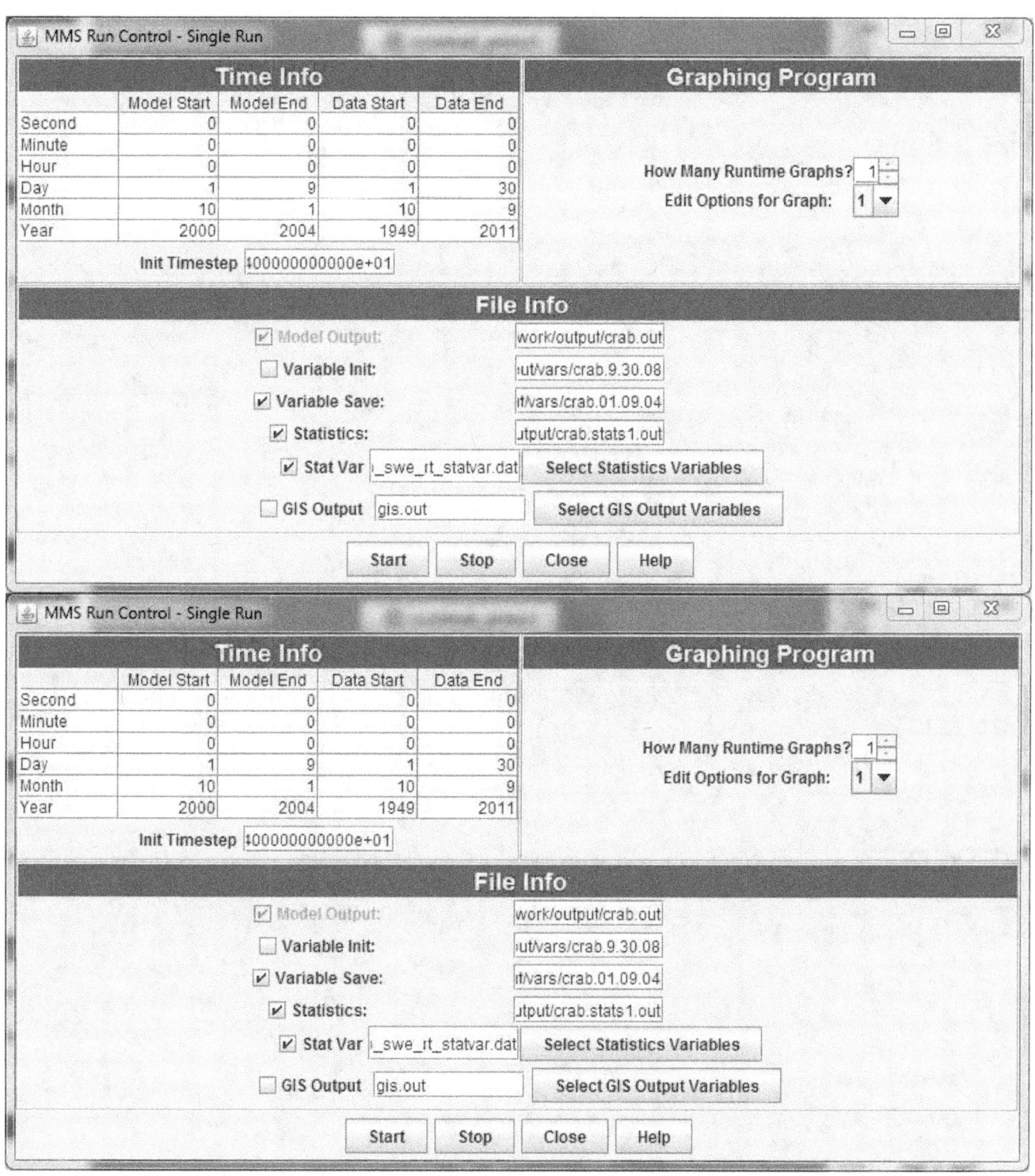

Figure 11. Screen capture of the MMS Run Control - Single Run window for the Modular Modeling System traditional user interface for the Crab Creek model, Potholes Reservoir basin, Washington.

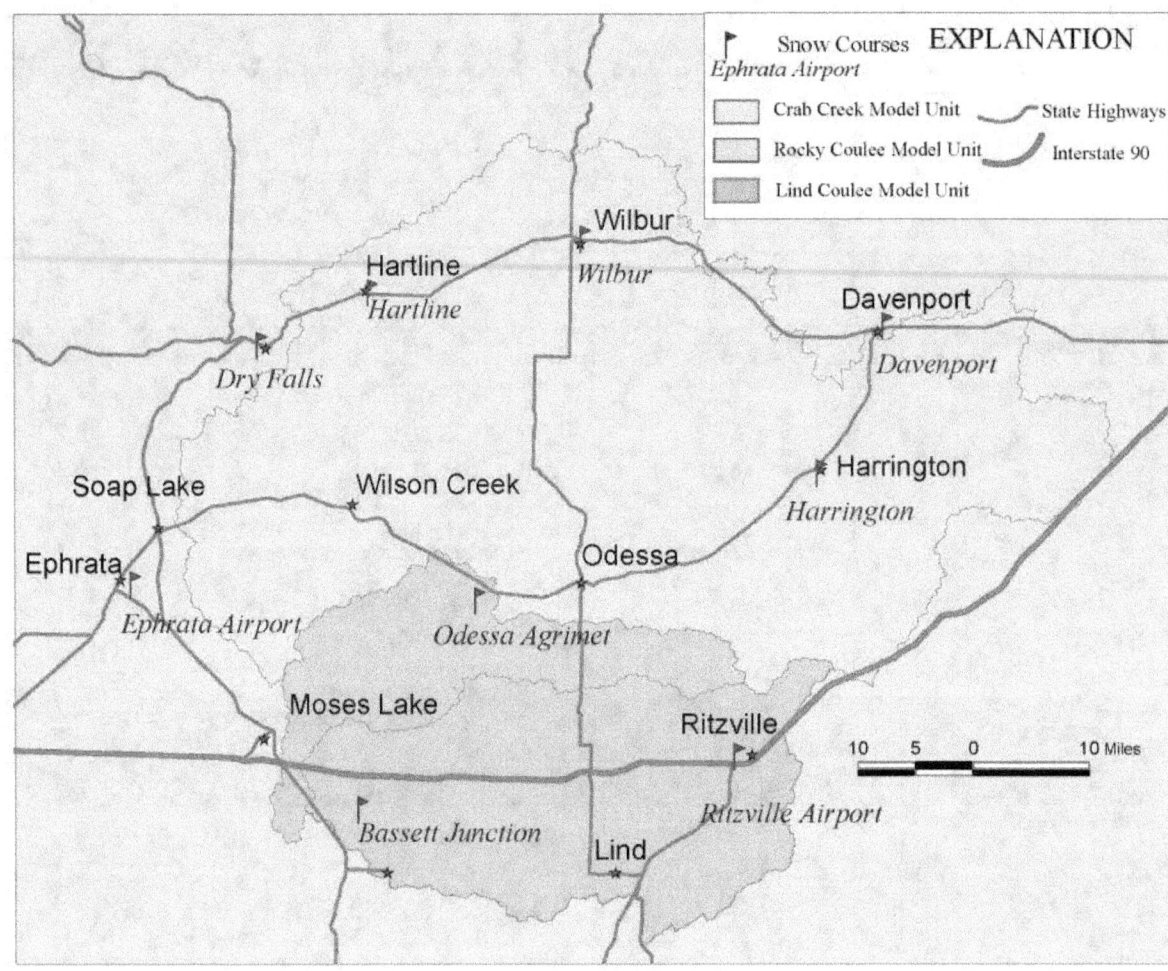

Figure 12.   Existing network of snow courses in and near the watershed model boundaries, Potholes Reservoir basin, Washington. Detailed descriptions of the snow courses are given in Appendix B.

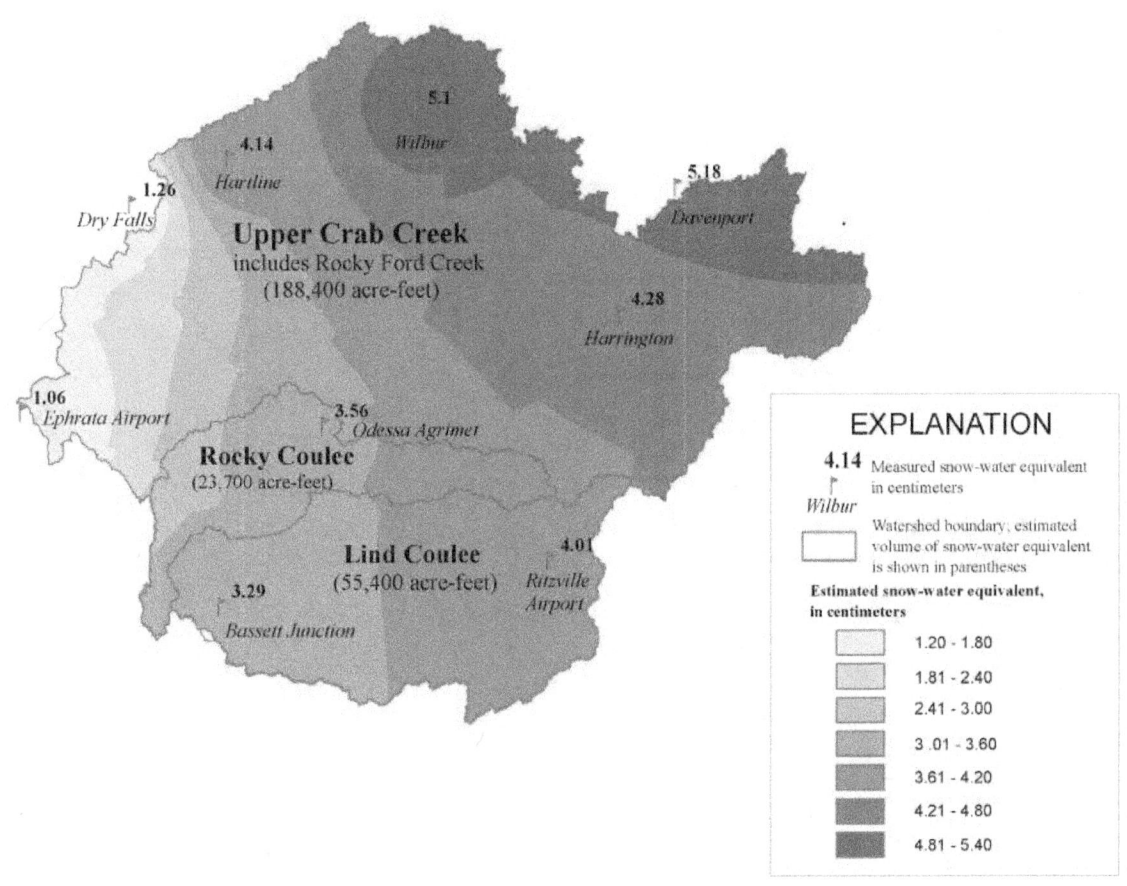

Figure 13. Snow-water equivalent measured at nine locations during January 8-9, 2004, and snow-water equivalent throughout the model domain estimated based on the measured values, Potholes Reservoir basin, Washington.

Crab Creek Snow Survey

Site_____ Date/Time_____

Surveyor_____ Weather_____

Air Temp._____

Average Depth_____ Soil Temp._____

Range of Densities_____

Average Snow-Water Equivalent (SWE)_____

Remarks_____

_____

[on one side of the field notebook]

Snow Depth

Station (ft)	Depth (cm)
1. _____	_____
2. _____	_____
3. _____	_____
4. _____	_____
5. _____	_____
6. _____	_____
7. _____	_____
8. _____	_____
9. _____	_____
10. _____	_____

[on the other side of the field notebook]

Snow Density

Weight (g)	Density (kg/m^3)	Depth Range (cm)	SWE (cm)	Temperature ($^{\circ}$C)
_____	_____	_____	_____	_____
_____	_____	_____	_____	_____
_____	_____	_____	_____	_____
_____	_____	_____	_____	_____
_____	_____	_____	_____	_____

Figure 14. A proposed field-sheet layout for collecting snow-survey information.

	A	B	C	D	E	F	G	H	I	J	K
1	Calculation of variables freeh2o, pk_ice and pk_depth										
2											
3	Sorted by HRU		from GIS_out		from variable file		=IF(E4=0,C4*0.02,0)		pkwater_equiv - freeh2o	density = 0.204	
4	CRAB_HR	XYXY021	pkwater_equiv		pk_temp		freeh2o		pk_ice	pk_depth	
5	1	418	4.180		0.00E+00		0.084		4.096	20.490	
6	2	400	4.000		0.00E+00		0.080		3.920	19.608	
7	3	405	4.050		0.00E+00		0.081		3.969	19.853	
8	4	420	4.200		0.00E+00		0.084		4.116	20.588	
9	5	433	4.330		0.00E+00		0.087		4.243	21.225	
10	6	399	3.990		0.00E+00		0.080		3.910	19.559	
11	7	410	4.100		0.00E+00		0.082		4.018	20.098	
12	8	426	4.260		0.00E+00		0.085		4.175	20.882	

Figure 15. Screen capture of spreadsheet used to calculate variables freeh2o, pk_ice, and pk_depth.

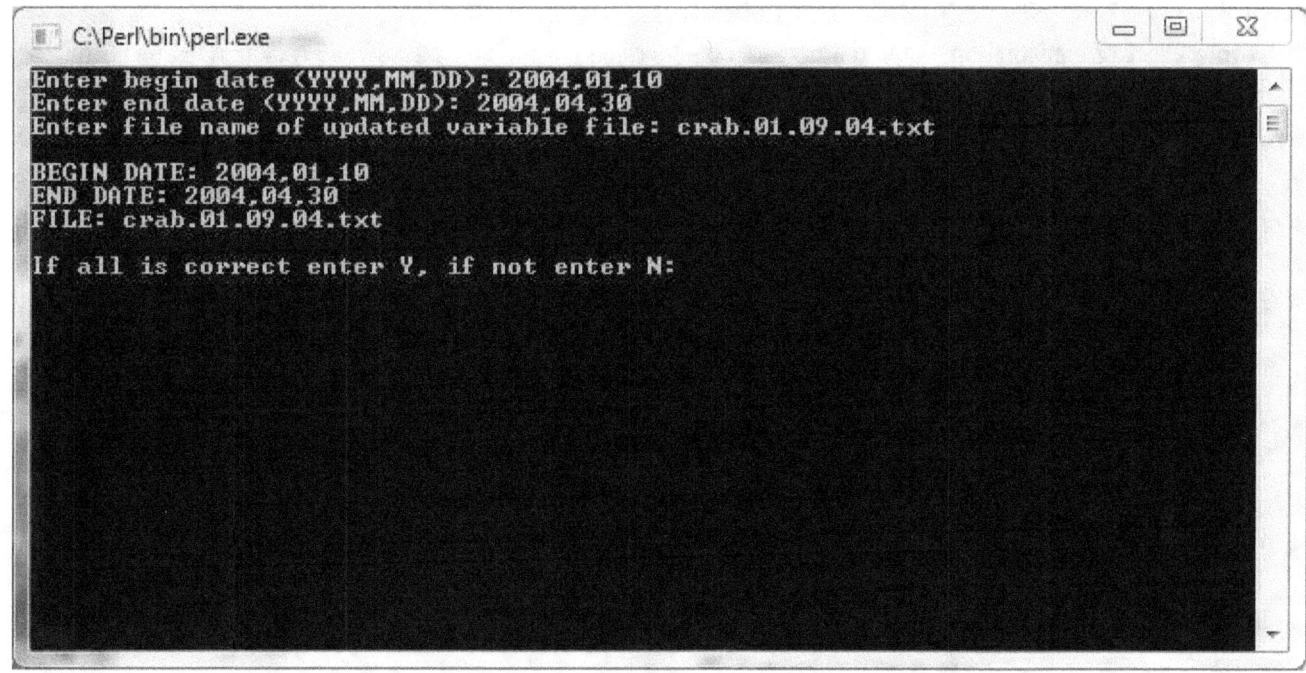

Figure 16. Screen capture of Ensemble Streamflow Prediction (ESP) update window with start and end date and variable file entered for the example ESP model run updated with snow-survey data.

Table 1. Comparison of measured runoff volumes and runoff volumes simulated with the 2012 model at three streamflow-gaging stations, upper Crab Creek basin, Washington, January 1-June 30, water years (WY) 2010-11.

Streamflow-gaging station	January-June, WY 2010			January-June, WY 2011		
	Measured runoff (acre-feet)	Simulated runoff (acre-feet)	Percent difference	Measured runoff (acre-feet)	Simulate runoff (acre-feet)	Percent difference
Crab Creek at Rocky Ford Road	21,889	7,196	-67.1	31,966	25,574	-20.0
Coal Creek at Mohler	2,538	147	-94.2	2,731	1,334	-51.2
Crab Creek at Irby	19,745	7,085	-64.1	26,761	32,466	21.3

Table 2. Comparison of measured runoff volumes and the Ensemble Streamflow Prediction (ESP) 50-percent-exceedance-probability runoff volumes generated by the 2009 and 2012 models at three streamflow-gaging stations, upper Crab Creek basin, Washington, for runoff season January 1-June 30, water years (WY) 2010-11.

Streamflow-gaging station	January 1 through June 30, WY 2010				January 1 through June 30, WY 2011			
	ESP 50-percent-exceedance-probability runoff volume, 2009 model (acre-feet)	ESP 50-percent-exceedance-probability runoff volume, 2012 model (acre-feet)	Measured runoff volume (acre-feet)	Percent difference between simulated and measured runoff volume, 2012 model	ESP 50-percent-exceedance-probability runoff volume, 2009 model (acre-feet)	ESP 50-percent-exceedance-probability runoff volume, 2012 model (acre-feet)	Measured runoff volume (acre-feet)	Percent difference between simulated and measured runoff volume, 2012 model
Crab Creek at Rocky Ford Road	17,636	15,806	21,889	-27.8	40,811	31,891	31,966	-0.2
Coal Creek at Mohlar	1,292	1,537	2,538	-39.4	3,496	3,171	2,731	16.1
Crab creek at Irby	21,400	20,224	19,745	2.4	48,283	42,888	26,761	60.3

Table 3. Meteorological sites, data sources, and sequence numbers indicating the order of data items in the input file for the real-time Potholes watershed model, Potholes Reservoir basin, Washington.

Meteorological Site	Data Source	Sequence Number		
		Daily Precipitation	Daily Minimum Temperature	Daily Maximum Temperature
Davenport	Hydromet	1	10	19
Ephrata AP	NWS	2	11	20
Harrington	NWS	3	12	21
Almira	Hydromet	4	13	22
Lind	Hydromet	5	14	23
Moses Lake	NWS	6	15	24
Odessa	Hydromet	7	16	25
Ritzville	NWS	8	17	26
Wilbur	NWS	9	18	27

Table 4. Point identification numbers and related snow-course names for the input file, sno_crs_pts.txt, used to generate a snow-water equivalent grid for the Potholes Reservoir basin, Washington.

POINT ID	Snow-Course Name
1	Ephrata
2	Dry Falls
3	Hartline
4	Wilber
5	Davenport
6	Harrington
7	Ritzville
8	Odessa
9	Bassett Junction

Table 5. Example of first six rows of data in the spreadsheet showing (A) GIS output; (B) values of snow-water equivalent (SWE), sorted by Hydrologic Response Unit (HRU); (C) imported area values that are used to compute SWE volume; and (D) SWE volume for each HRU.

	from Jan 04 GIS output		Sorted by HRU		Hru_area		SWE volume
Record	CRAB HRU	XYXY027	CRAB HRU	XYXY027, inches	HRU	Area, acres	in ac-ft
1	11	458	1	4.18	1	4965.59	1729.68
2	50	500	2	4	2	3260.50	1086.833
3	12	485	3	4.05	3	1164.35	392.9681
4	15	503	4	4.2	4	1886.63	660.3205
5	13	492	5	4.33	5	1560.15	562.9541
6	16	504	6	3.99	6	6305.93	2096.722

Appendix A. Potholes Watershed Model Background

Three modeling units in the Potholes watershed-modeling project are simulated in separate models: Crab Creek (21 flow-routing nodes), Rocky Coulee (11 flow-routing nodes), and Lind Coulee (14 flow-routing nodes). All models use the executable file PRMSIV_dev.exe and the same data file, either pot_rt.data (water years 1950-current) or pot_lt.data (water years 1950-2004). The long term data file (pot_lt.data) has nine weather-station inputs and the real-time data file (pot_rt.data) has seven weather-station inputs (with some different stations) and missing values (-9999.00) for the other two stations. All weather stations measure maximum and minimum daily temperature and daily precipitation. The Potholes Object User Interface (OUI) has been set up to allow the user to run long-term model runs (Single Run) and to get the simulated discharge time series at all 46 flow-routing nodes for the three models. The OUI also includes the ability to run real-time Ensemble Streamflow Prediction (ESP) model runs and generate output at nine specific nodes. All the runoff routing is done within the PRMSIV_dev.exe executable between flow-routing nodes (fig. A1, table A1).

Appendix B. Snow-Course Locations

The hand-drawn maps and photographs included in this appendix provide additional location information about the proposed network of nine snow courses. Refer to figure 12 in the main text for the general location of these snow courses. Latitude and longitude of the snow-course locations are included in the hand-drawn maps. The hand-drawn maps and photographs were made during a snow survey during January 8-9, 2004. The snow-water equivalents measured at nine locations are shown in figure 13.

The following are hand-drawn maps and some topographic maps for the nine snow-course locations (fig. 12), listed in alphabetical order:
1. Bassett Junction
2. Davenport
3. Dry Falls
4. Ephrata Airport
5. Harrington
6. Hartline
7. Odessa Agrimet
8. Ritzville Airport
9. Wilbur

Bassett Junction Sno Course

Located on N. side of rd 3SE and E side
of RR Tracks. Just on E side of intersection
of RR Tracks and 3SE there is a primitive
dirt rd. snow course parallels this road
on E side.

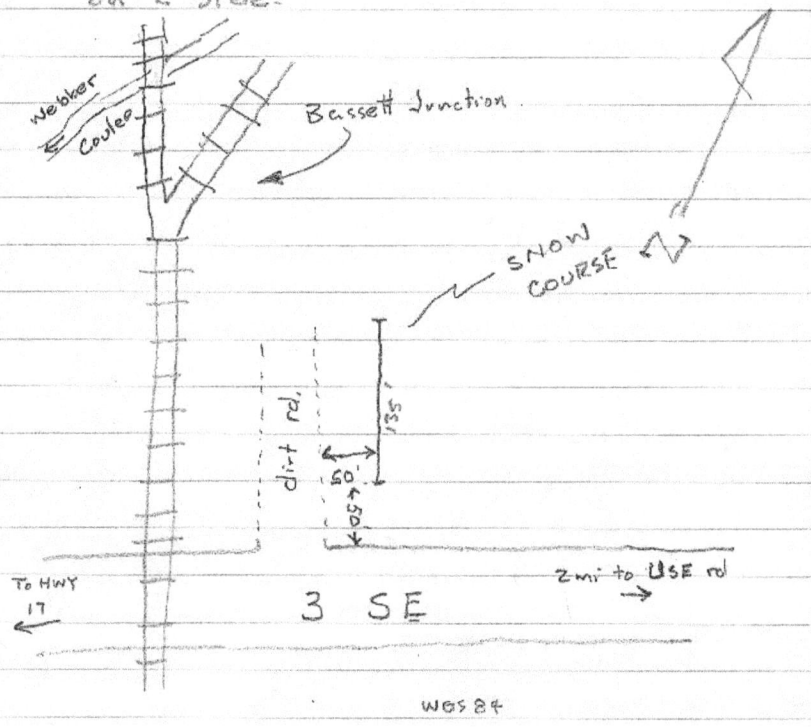

Webber Coulee

Bassett Junction

SNOW COURSE

dirt rd.

35'

50'

50'

To HWY 17

3 SE

2 mi to USE rd →

WGS 84

took pics 107 - 109

N 47° 02' 30.1"   EPE = 15'

W 119° 05' 17.2"

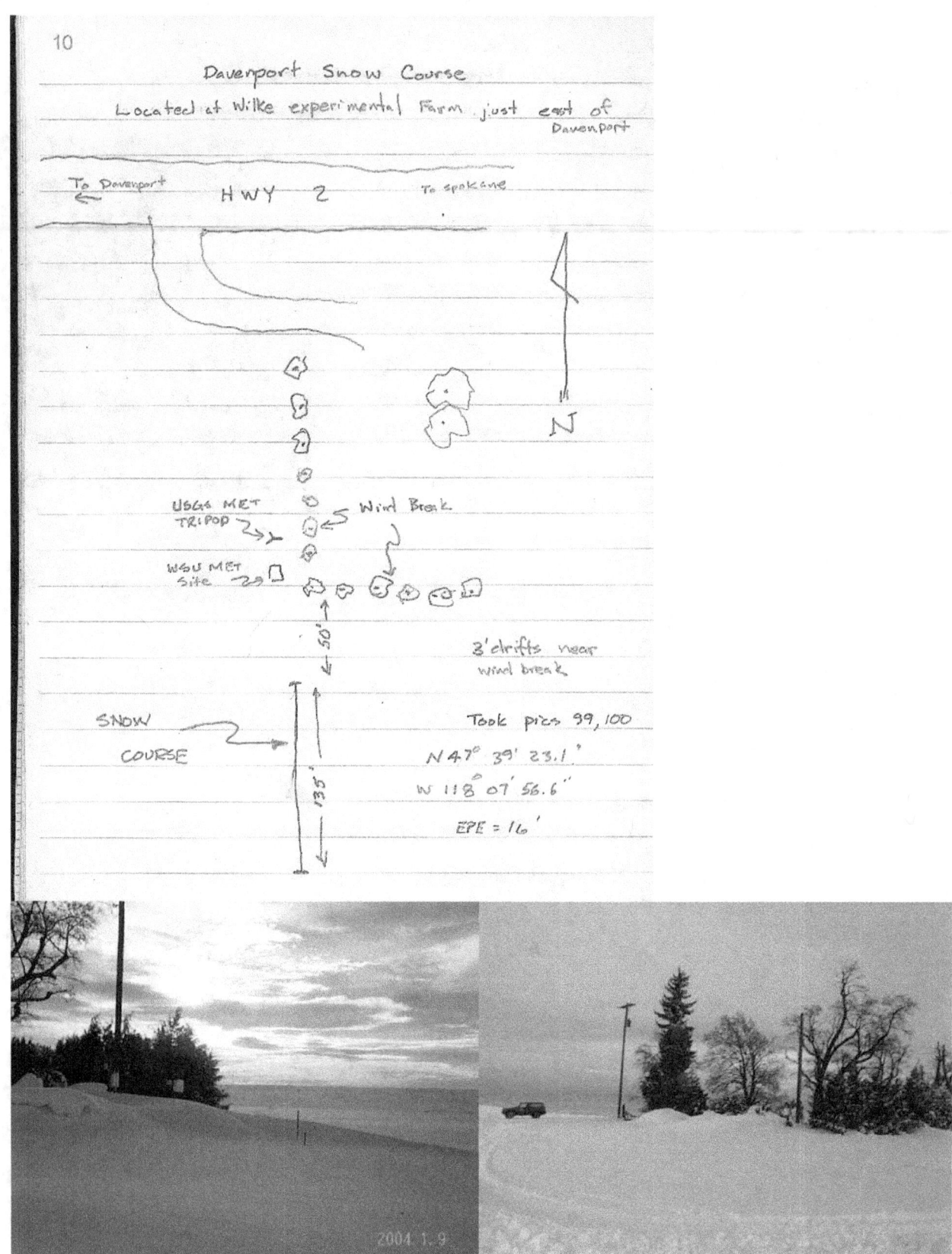

Davenport Snow Course

Located at Wilke experimental Farm just east of Davenport

To Davenport ← HWY 2   To Spokane

N

USGS MET TRIPOD →

Wind Break

WSU MET Site

← 50' →

← 135' →

SNOW COURSE →

3' drifts near wind break

Took pics 99, 100

N 47° 39' 23.1"

W 118° 07' 56.6"

EPE = 16'

2004 1.9

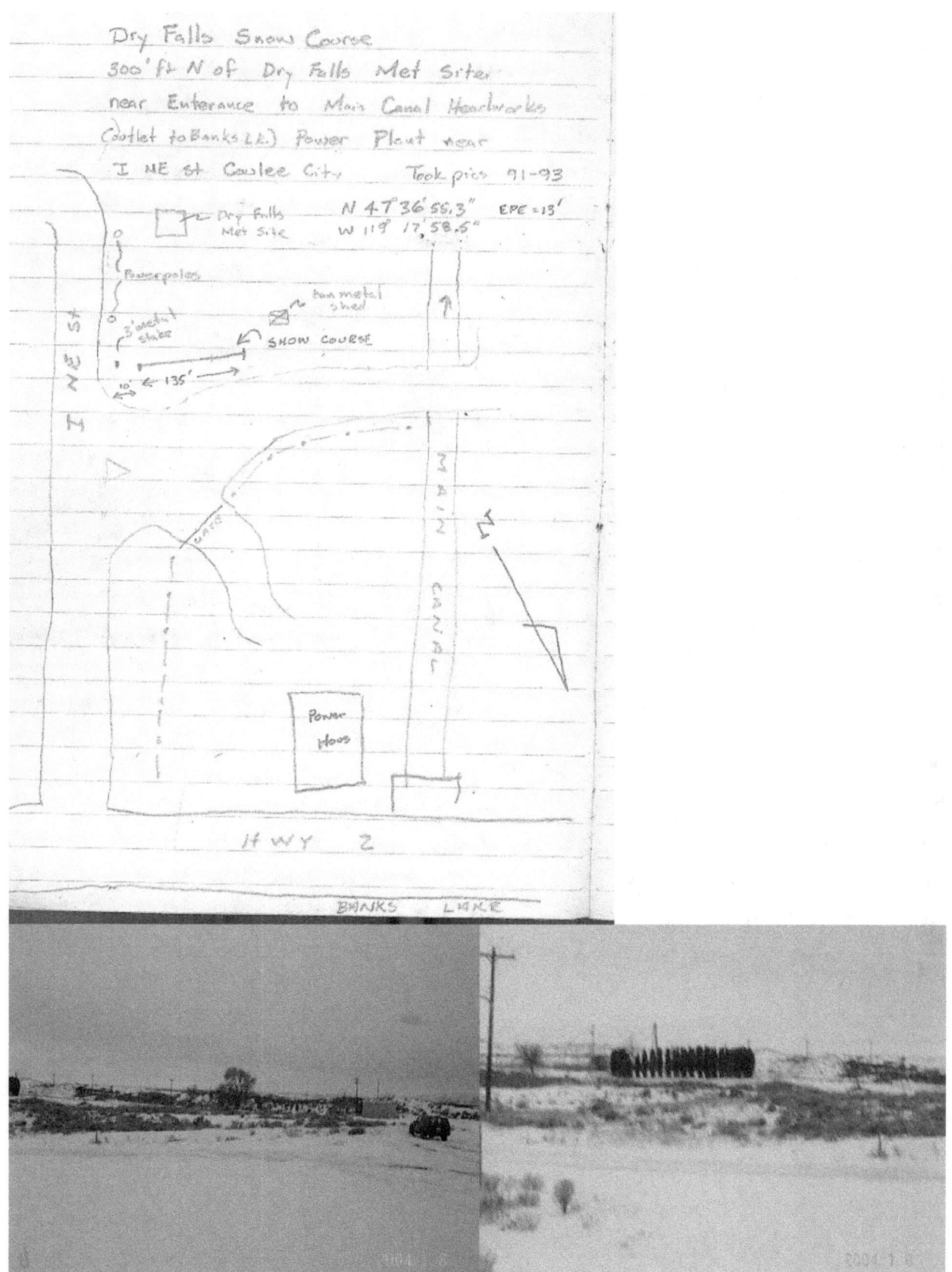

Ephrata Airport Snow Course
at corner of E Division & Airport Rd
near enterace to airport

N 47° 18' 45.5"   EPE = 12 ft

W 119 31 18.7"   WGS 84 datum

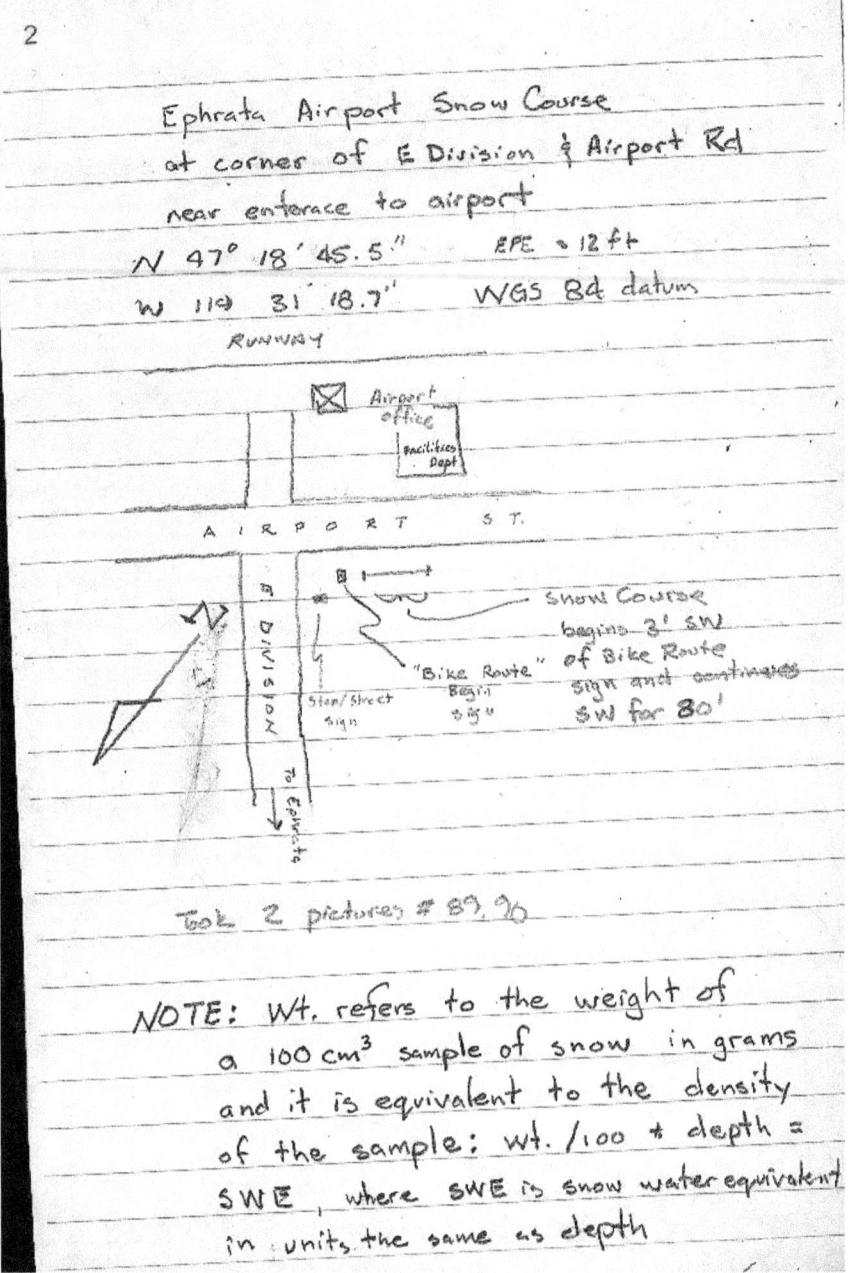

Took 2 pictures # 89, 90

NOTE: Wt. refers to the weight of
a 100 cm³ sample of snow in grams
and it is equivalent to the density
of the sample; wt./100 * depth =
SWE, where SWE is snow water equivalent
in units the same as depth

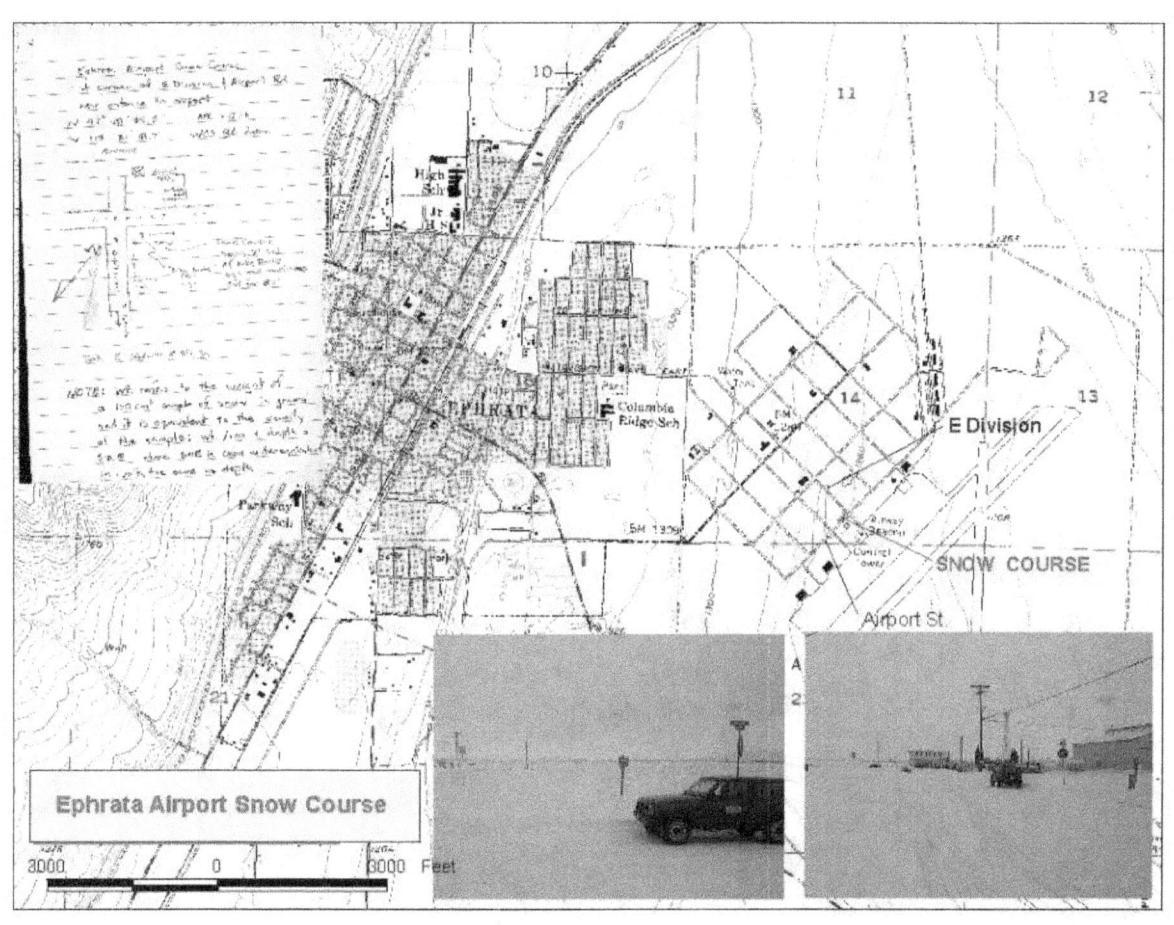

Ephrata Airport Snow Course

3000   0   3000 Feet

E Division

SNOW COURSE

Airport St.

12

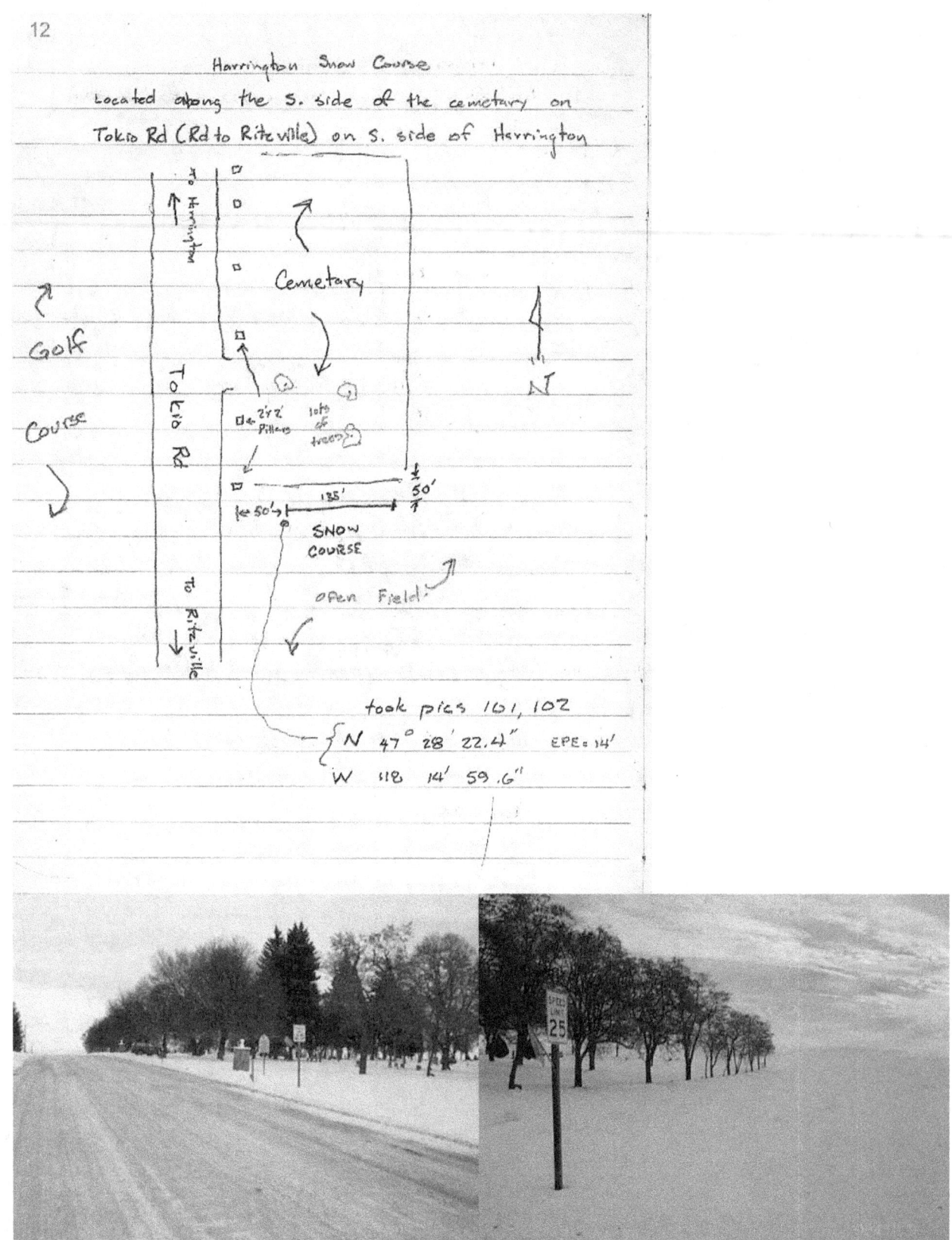

Harrington Snow Course

Located along the S. side of the cemetary on
Tokio Rd (Rd to Riteville) on S. side of Harrington

to Harrington

Golf
Course

Tokio Rd

to Riteville

Cemetary

N

2'x2'
Pillars

lots
of
trees

50'

135'

50'

50'

SNOW
COURSE

open Field

took pics 101, 102

N 47° 28' 22.4"   EPE: 14'

W 118 14' 59.6"

Hartline Snow Course

Located at cemetary on S. side Hwy 2
½ mi east of school. Snow course along east
fence line beginning 10 ft s. of Power pole
running due S 135 ft 10' away from fence

Took pics 94,955

N 47°41' 04.6"   EPE = 15'

W 119°05' 39.2"

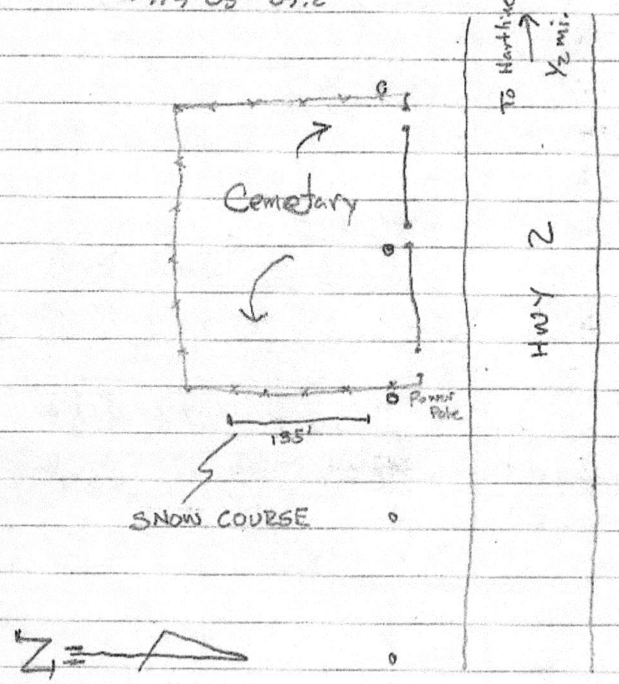

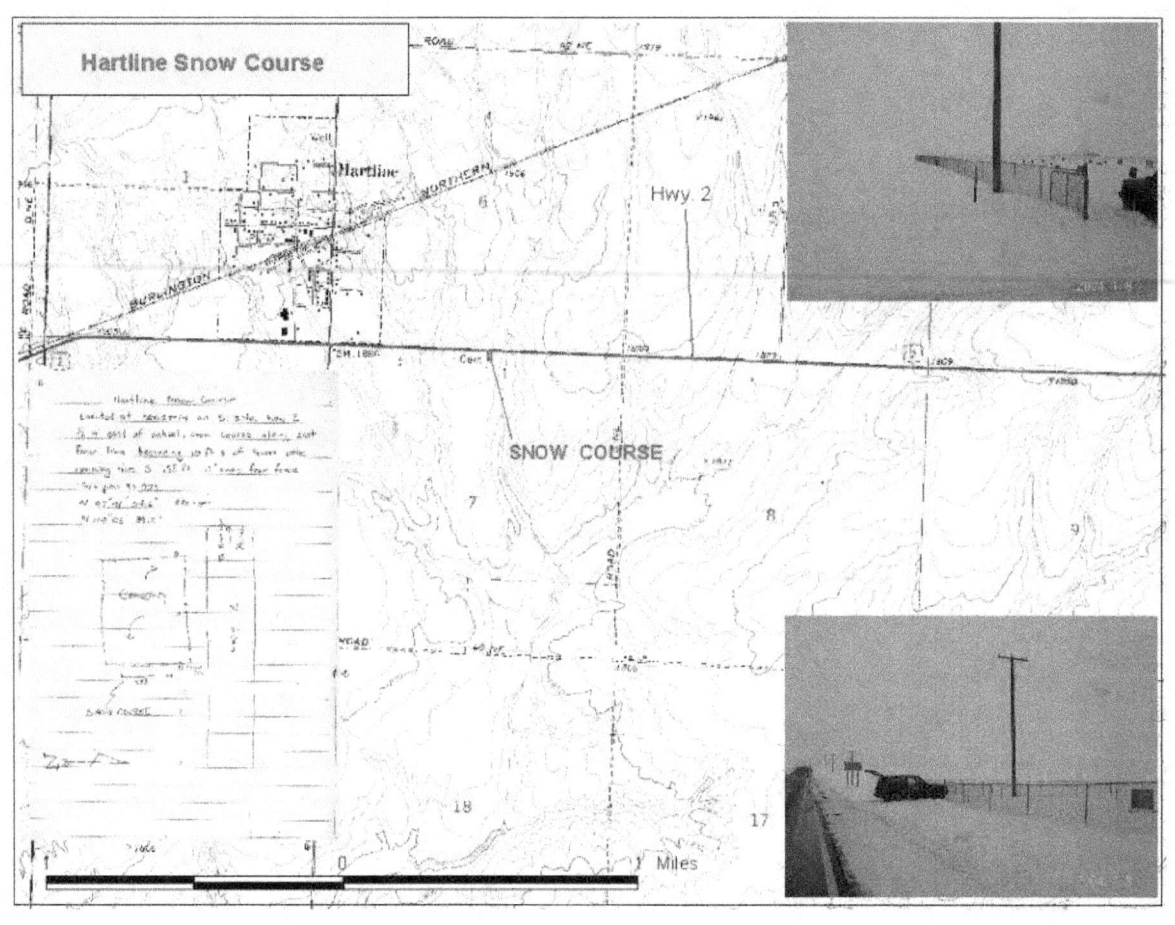

ODESSA Agrimet Site Sno Course

Located on access rd to Agrimet site ~1000 ft
S. of site nr intersection w/Bates Rd. Go west
8mi from Odessa on Hwy 28 turn rt on
Kagele, go 1.0mi turn rt. on Bates, go 1.2 mi
to privat drive

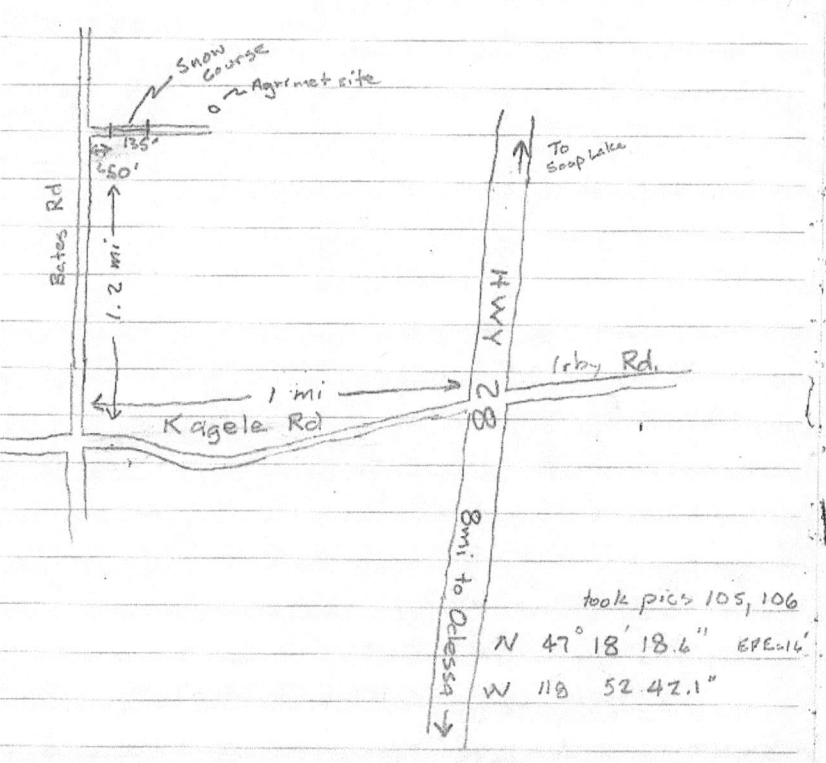

took pics 105, 106

N 47° 18' 18.6"   EPE=16'

W 118 52.42.1"

Ritzville Airport Snow Course

Located at S. end of runway at Pru Field

near parallel to Weber Rd, perpenticular to runway

N 47° 07' 05.9" EPE = 12'

W 118° 23' 35.7"

took pic

Wilbur Snow Course

Located in Emerson Park just East of
town on S. side of Hwy 2. Snow course begins
at home plate on baseball diamond facing Hwy 2
goes 135' down 1ST base line

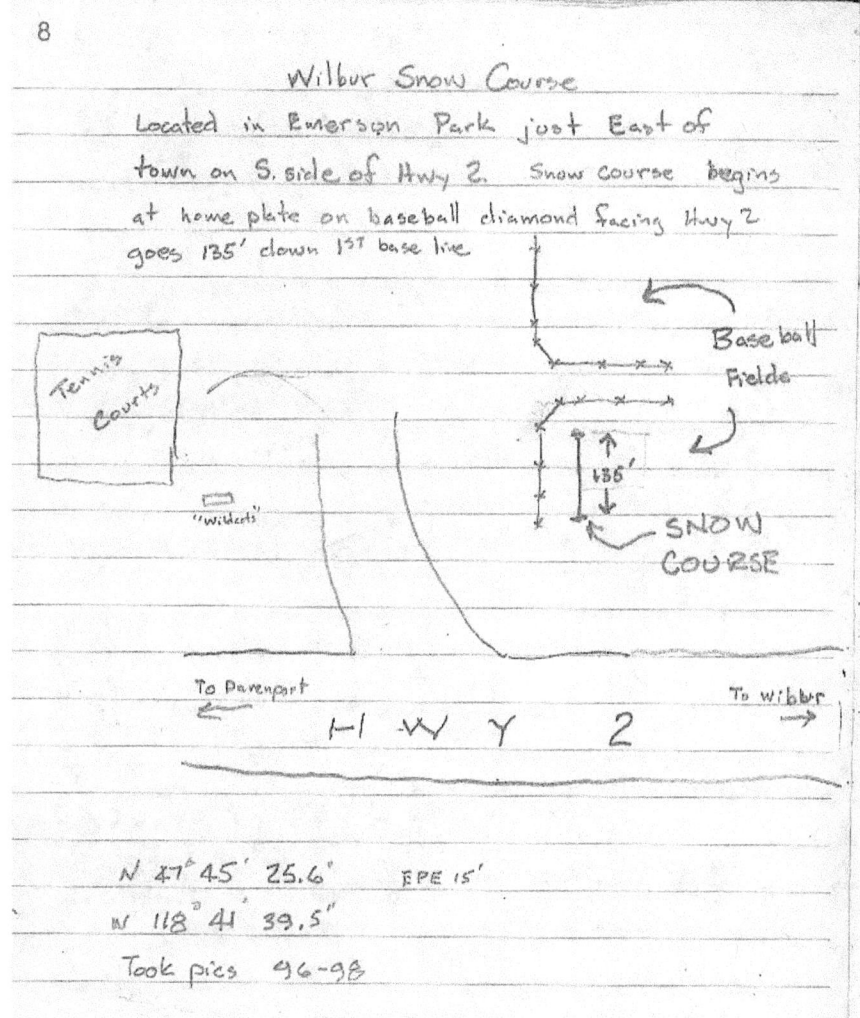

N 47° 45' 25.6'   EPE 15'

W 118° 41' 39.5"

Took pics 96-98

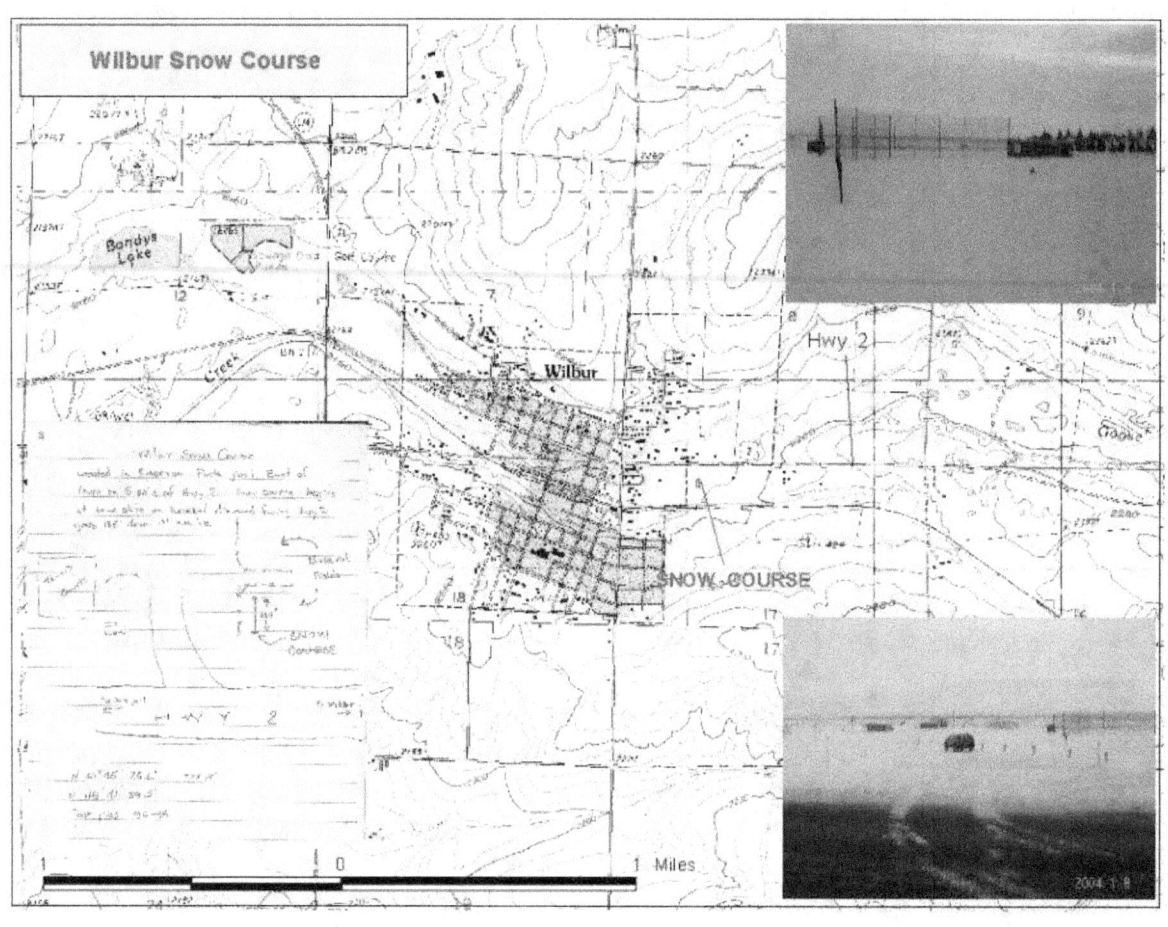

Appendix figure and table:

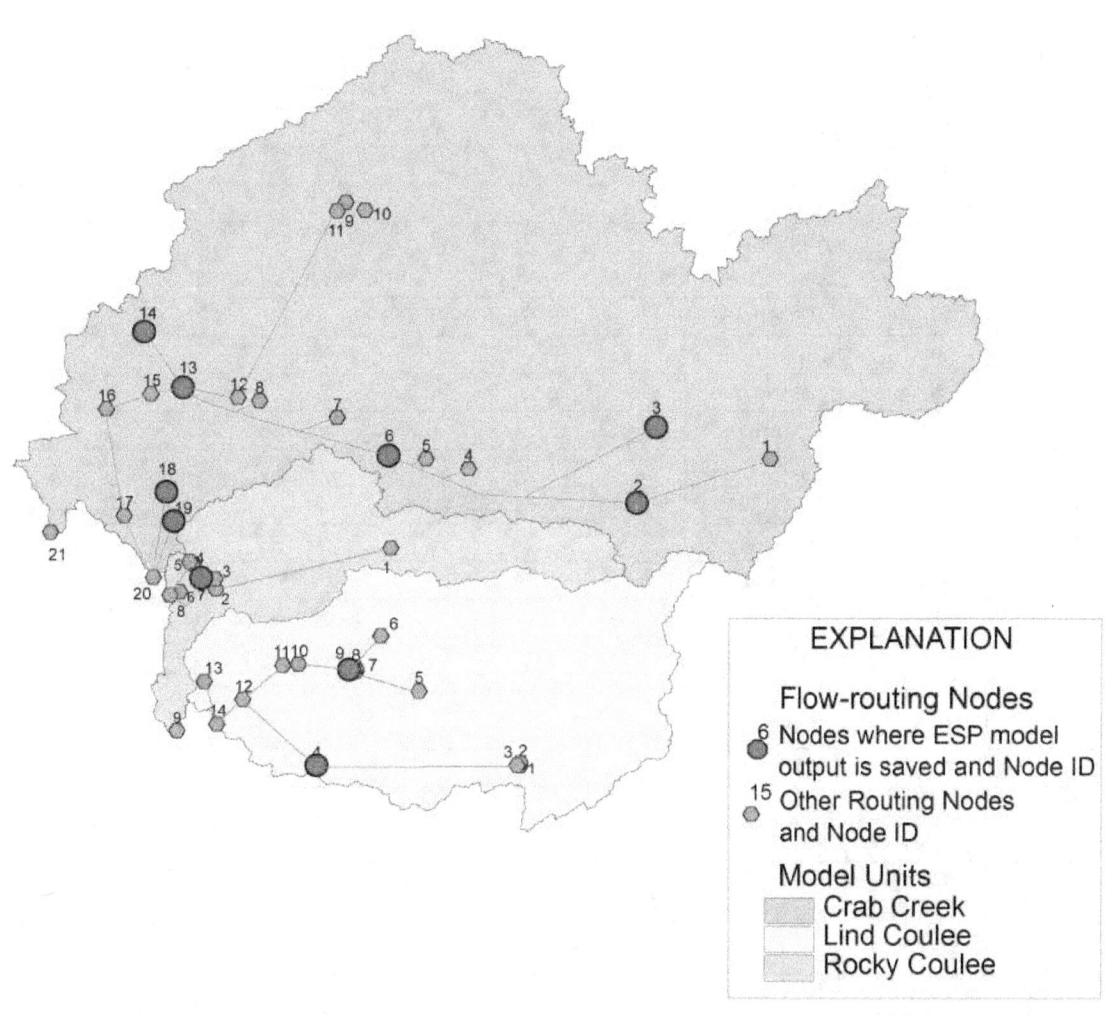

Figure A1. Potholes model units and flow-routing nodes.

Table A1. Flow-routing nodes.

Node ID	Model	Subbasin	USGS streamflow-gaging station and number
1	Crab	Crab abv. Lords	
2	Crab	Crab abv Rockyford Rd	
3	Crab	Coal Creek	Coal Creek at Mohler, 12464800
4	Crab	Duck Creek	
5	Crab	Lake Creek	
6	Crab	Odessa	Crab Creek at Irby, 1246500
7	Crab	Martin Hollow	
8	Crab	Canniwai	
9	Crab	Corbett	
10	Crab	Upper Wilson	
11	Crab	Corbett + Upper Wilson	Wilson Creek blw Corbett Draw, 12465400
12	Crab	Wilson	
13	Crab	Stratford	
14	Crab	Arbuckle	
15	Crab	Below Brooks Lake	
16	Crab	Upper Irrigated	
17	Crab	Middle Irrigated	
18	Crab	Broken Rock	
19	Crab	Black Lake	
20	Crab	Crab near Moses Lake	Crab Creek near Moses Lake, 1246700
21	Crab	Rocky Ford	
1	Rocky	Upper Rocky	
2	Rocky	Rocky	
3	Rocky	Cemetary	
4	Rocky	Sand	
5	Rocky	Black Rock	
6	Rocky	Block 40	
7	Rocky	Rocky at East Low Canal	
8	Rocky	Rocky near mouth	
9	Rocky	Block 41	
10	Rocky	Block 42 trib	
11	Rocky	Block 42	
1	Lind	McElroy Coulee	
2	Lind	Paha Coulee	
3	Lind	Upper Lind	
4	Lind	Lind Coulee	
5	Lind	Bauer Coulee	
6	Lind	Farrier Coulee	Farrier Coulee near Schrag, 12471270
7	Lind	Upper Weber Coulee	

8	Lind	Farrier at mouth	
9	Lind	Weber	
10	Lind	North Fork	
11	Lind	Mid-Weber	
12	Lind	Lower Lind	
13	Lind	Lower Lind-North	
14	Lind	Lind near mouth	Lind Coulee Wasteway at SR17, 12471400